Cognitive
Psychology

SAGE COURSE COMPANIONS

KNOWLEDGE AND SKILLS *for* SUCCESS

Cognitive Psychology

Carol Brown

SAGE Publications

London • Thousand Oaks • New Delhi

First published 2006

SAGE Publications Ltd
1 Oliver's Yard
55 City Road
London EC1Y 1SP

SAGE Publications Inc.
2455 Teller Road
Thousand Oaks, California 91320

SAGE Publications India Pvt Ltd
B-42, Panchsheel Enclave
Post Box 4109
New Delhi 110 017

British Library Cataloguing in Publication data

A catalogue record for this book is available from the British Library

ISBN-10 1-4129-1838-3   ISBN-13 978-1-4129-1838-1
ISBN-10 1-4129-1839-1 (pbk)   ISBN-13 978-1-4129-1839-8 (pbk)

Library of Congress Control Number: 2006929609

Typeset by C&M Digitals (P) Ltd., Chennai, India
Printed in Great Britain by The Cromwell Press Ltd, Trowbridge, Wiltshire
Printed on paper from sustainable resources

To Dr Sally Hope without whose suggestion I would not be writing my fifth book and more importantly, for her unfailing support which has kept our little family going in the last few years

contents

<table>
<tr><td>

introduction

</td><td></td></tr>
</table>

Why Use this Course Companion to Cognitive Psychology?

This book is designed to help you succeed on your degree level psychology course. The aim is to provide you with a course companion that gives you a short cut to understanding the basics behind cognitive psychology. It is about helping you to gain the most from your degree level course, pass your examinations in psychology and achieve success in your assignments.

It has been designed and written to provide you, the reader, with an easy-to-navigate guide to the commonly taught curriculum in cognitive psychology, and the ways of thinking and writing that your examiners will be looking for when they start to grade your work.

This companion is not to be used instead of a textbook or wider reading, but rather as a means of memorising content and familiarising oneself with the basics of the discipline when preparing for an examination or planning an assessment essay. The book will help you to structure and organise your thoughts, and will enable you to get the most from your textbooks and the other reading that you will do as part of your course. This companion is designed to point you in the direction of key thinkers and key ideas, and to give you the briefest of introductions to their work and how to put their work in context. It will also point you in the direction of the most important readings and thinkers, and will encourage you to widen your reading and research so as to improve your attainment.

This guide therefore provides you with ways of applying the information that you are familiar with in a practical manner, and is aimed at ensuring that you gain the skills necessary to convey your theoretical/academic material successfully.

As you are still relatively new to the study of psychology you may assume that simply learning the material presented in lectures secures high achievement, but actually the learning and rewriting of information will not gain you top marks. Instead, you need to go beyond simply understanding the material to think critically about the research presented to you. This ability to evaluate theories/studies is the essential skill from which a psychologist derives success.

How to Use this Book

This companion should be used as a supplement to your textbook and lecture notes. You may want to glance through it quickly, reading it in parallel with your course syllabus and textbook, and note where each topic is covered in both the syllabus and this companion. Ideally, you should have already obtained this book before your course starts, so that you can get a quick overview of each topic before you go into the lecture, but if you didn't do this, all is not lost. The companion will still be equally helpful as a revision guide, and as a way of directing you towards the key thinkers and theories in cognitive psychology.

Part One is about how to think like a cognitive psychologist: it will help you to get into the mindset of the subject and think about it critically. As a bonus, of course, it also means learning how to think like your examiner! Examiners want to see that you can handle the basic concepts of your subject: if you need a quick overview of the background to cognitive psychology, this is the section you will find most useful.

Part Two goes into the curriculum in more detail, taking each topic and providing you with the key elements. Again, this does not substitute the deeper coverage you will have had in your lectures and texts, but it does provide a quick revision guide, or a 'primer' to use before lectures.

You can also use this book either to give yourself a head start before you begin studying cognitive psychology – in other words, give yourself a preview course – or it can be used as a revision aid, or, of course, both. Each section contains within it the following features:

- **Tips** on handling the information in exams, or reminders of key issues. This will help you to anticipate exam questions, and help you to remember the main points to bring in when answering them.
- **Examples** that are useful for putting theory into a 'real world' context and can, of course, be used in exams to illustrate the points you make.
- **Running themes** of the areas that will always be of interest to a cognitive psychologist. You will find that these can almost always be brought into an exam question, and you will be expected to do so.
- Input from **key thinkers** in the field, which will be useful to quote in exams, as well as providing you with the main influences and theories within cognitive psychology.

- Sample **exam questions** with outline **answers**. These should help you to be better prepared for the actual questions, even though they will, of course, be different.
- The **Textbook guide** is about taking your thinking a stage further by introducing some texts which focus on academic thinking. This will help you to take a broader conceptual view of the topic; on a practical level, this is the type of thinking that moves you from a pass to a first!

Part Three is a study guide which will help you with getting more from your lectures, to remember more when you are sitting exams, and to write essays.

Following the main text is a glossary of the key terms that are used in the book and a list of references.

part one

the basics of cognitive psychology

The overall aim of Part One is to familiarise you with the basics of cognitive psychology. It will:

- define cognitive psychology as a topic
- look at cognitive psychology and its related disciplines
- give you a brief history of cognitive psychology
- introduce the founding figures and their core ideas
- encourage you to think like a cognitive psychologist
- help you to understand the general principles of assessment and expected learning outcomes when studying this area of psychology
- provide tips and examples of the running themes you will find throughout the forthcoming text.

1.1	
definition	

Cognitive psychology deals with topics such as perception, memory, attention, language and thinking/decision making. Most critically it is based on the idea that we are like a computer when processing information and have an input, storage and retrieval function. Experimental cognitive psychology presumes that cognitive processes can be tested using empirical (scientific) methods because they can be inferred from behaviour obtained under controlled conditions. Introspection can, however, also be used whereby one examines one's own mental processes.

One should bear in mind, however, that only indirect information can be obtained from internal processes and artificial laboratory environments, and that people are usually unaware of their own mental processes, although introspection can be useful when describing an event rather than interpreting it.

Cognitive psychology assumes we are just like computers and that we process information using input, storage and retrieval processes.

1.2	
cognitive psychology and related disciplines/theories	

Experimental cognitive psychology

Places an experimental emphasis on cognitive psychology.

Cognitive science

Uses computational/computer models to understand cognitions. It allows specification of a theory to predict behaviour. Flowcharts are used to construct theories and provide a plan from which input can be examined as well as the nature of storage and decision processes. This information can then be used to devise a computer program.

The interaction of psychological theory with programming is a difficult one and the relationship between the performance of a program and human participation may be different: for example, programs may run faster.

There are three main types of computational modelling techniques:

1 **Semantic networks:** where concepts are linked by a network of nodes that represent general (associative/similar) relationships, specific relationships or complete ones. The strength of these links will vary according to the similarity of different concepts, and learning occurs when new links are added or the strength of the relationship changes.

2 **Production changes:** these are made up of rules ('if ... then ...') that are held in the long-term memory of a production system that also contains a working memory where information that is being processed is held. The system operates by matching such processed information with the 'if' part of the rule to produce the appropriate 'then' response. Strategies are also used to select the most appropriate response.

3 **Connectionist networks:** these use modelling techniques that suggest networks have structures and layers which are connected together (like neurons/nodes). Concepts are stored within the network and are activated by patterns, which are simply the associations between inputs and outputs, and especially important is back-propogation, which uses a comparison of actual and correct responses.

Cognitive neuropsychology

Looks at impaired cognitive processes (for example, brain damage) in order to understand normal cognitions. It uses dissociations and is useful because it allows us to see the processes and mechanics involved in normal cognitive functioning. There is, however, a problem with using single dissociations, as a good performance on one task rather than another may simply be due to confounding variables, such as task complexity, and it is therefore better to look at double dissociations, that is, compare impaired performance on tasks between different patients. Theoretical assumptions of this model include the following: the idea that cognitive systems are modular; the brain and mind are related with specific functions in specific areas of the brain; and impaired cognitive functioning can tell us much about normal cognitive functioning.

When evaluating theoretical assumptions you should always bear in mind that:

- as modules don't actually exist physically, this presents difficulties
- much of the work is based on case studies that are difficult to generalise.

Cognitive neuroscience

Looks at brain functioning using biological techniques to understand human cognitions. For example, single-unit recording looks at the working of single neurons and is a sensitive technique that examines electrical changes; an EEG (electroencephalograph) uses electrodes attached to the scalp to detect small changes in electrical activity in the brain, while a PET (position emision tomography) scan can detect positrons emitted from radioactive water injected into the human body; and magnetic resonance imaging (MRI) measures radio waves that when excited by atoms produce magnetic changes detected by magnets – a computer then interprets these changes and produces 3-D images.

When considering the above approaches, keep it in mind that:

- these may be useful for providing detailed information about neural activity but can be invasive techniques
- they do not necessarily identify specific regions of parts of the brain, as the skull and tissue distort pictures
- rapid changes are difficult to identify and only provide an indirect measure of neural activity.

Often these approaches aren't distinctive and overlap.

1.3	
history of cognitive psychology	

In any examination or essay you will be expected to know something about where cognitive psychology comes from. This may simply be a matter of demonstrating a general understanding or not getting your origins muddled, but you may well be asked to write directly on the history of the discipline.

Understanding something of the history of cognitive psychology will be crucial in helping you think like a cognitive psychologist.

Key Developments

The years 1956 and 1957 were key dates in the development of cognitive psychology as several important papers/theories emerged including:

- Chomsky's theory of language
- Miller's concept of seven, plus or minus two chunks in short-term memory
- Newell & Simon's general problem-solving model
- Bruner et al.'s ideas on concept formation
- artificial intelligence (AI).

The **1970s** saw a further series of vital developments, especially the idea that the information-processing paradigm was the best way in which to study people/human cognition. It made several key assumptions, most notably that:

- people interact purposefully within the world
- patterns/symbols that are used in such interactions are made meaningful in the real-world context
- the processes and patterns used in performing cognitive tasks can be identified by psychologists and there is some neurological basis, although this does not control all information processing
- cognitive tasks may take time before being completed, although the mind has a limited-capacity processor.

1.4
founding figures and their core ideas

Inevitably, much of the discussion in this section concerning the founding figures and their core ideas overlaps with the preceding section detailing the history of the discipline. Core ideas had either a philosophical influence (their ideas and beliefs impacted on thinking about cognitive psychology) or a methodological influence (their ways of working and research studies influenced the development and thinking about cognitive psychology).

Atkinson & Shiffrin (1968) – multistore model of memory

A model of memory which assumes that there are three separate memory stores – sensory memory (SM), short-term memory (STM) and long-term memory (LTM), that information must flow from one store to the next, and that it can only be retained in STM if rehearsal has taken place.

Baddeley & Hitch (1974) – working memory model

This model comprises the *central executive,* which is a control system that is modality free and has a limited capacity; *the phonological loop,* which has an articulatory control system (verbal rehearsal, time-based, inner voice) and a phonological store (speech-based storage system, inner ear); and the *visuo-spatial scratch pad* ('inner eye'), which is designed for temporary storage and manipulation of spatial and visual information.

Broadbent (1958) – filter theory

The assumptions of filter theory are that two similar stimuli gain parallel access to a sensory register that briefly holds the information; a selective filter then allows one input through on the basis of physical characteristics and the other channel rests in the buffer. This is followed by some limited capacity processing and an output response. The importance of the filter, therefore, is that it prevents overload.

Treisman (1960) – attenuation theory

Assumes that the non-attended input is not rejected but is 'attenuated' (diminished) compared to attended information. All attenuated channels are then analysed semantically (that is, information is selected for its meaning) and information that has personal, important or current relevance is recognised thus making an output response possible.

Gibson (1950, 1966, 1979) – direct, bottom-up theory of perception

According to Gibson, perception is bottom-up (influenced by environmental stimuli) and direct. Perception results from sensation initially derived from the optic array, which picks up consistent information from the environment and does so even when there is interaction with different aspects of the environment (the consistency being referred to as invariants). Since this means that light is reaching the eye, it allows perception of depth, location and so on. Resonance aids the process whereby environmental stimuli are picked up and tuned into as an automatic process. Information thus takes the form of optic flow patterns (giving information on speed and direction of movement), texture gradients (closer objects seen in more detail than further ones) and affordances (detail about the function of objects).

Gregory (1972) – indirect, constructivist,
top-down theory of processing

This theory predicts that perception is an active process that is based on experience and expectations. Thus schemas (past knowledge, expectations and so on) make inferences about perceptual data. Perceptual constancies and illusions support this notion, that is, the size, shape and location of objects remain the same even when they are seen from different distances, angles and locations because the brain uses schemas to compensate for these changes and interprets on the basis of experience and expectations. A similar process occurs with illusions, of which there are numerous. To give just some examples, this process applies to distortions, ambiguous figures, paradoxical figures and fictions. Perceptual set is therefore also important. This is where previous experience, expectations, motivation and emotion create a bias towards the perception of particular stimuli (or aspects of it) whilst ignoring other available data.

Marr (1982) – computational theory

According to this model, individuals construct and then work through three hierarchical stages of representation before being able to recognise an object. An initial (retinal) representation (described by Marr as having two phases: 'the raw primal sketch', which recognises various light intensities; and 'the full primal sketch', which outlines shapes) provides basic information about the features of the object to form a 2.5-D sketch. At the second stage of representation, individuals interpret the 2.5-D from their own particular point of view. Finally, at the third stage, binocular disparity enables individuals to process more detailed information about the object, for example, depth (using the range map) and orientation, and subsequently construct a 3-D model based on the simple construction of an image (accessibility), its scope and uniqueness, and the similarities shared by and differences between objects (stability and sensitivity) (Marr & Nishihara, 1978).

1.5

thinking like a cognitive psychologist

The key to success in your cognitive psychology module is to learn how to think like a cognitive psychologist, including how to speak the language of academic psychology, using their terms and phrases in a relevant way, and understanding how to make links between topics and common themes. This book will give you hints and tips to guide you. It will ensure that you become confident about when and how to use this language and the ways of thinking about the world that come with this language.

The first section introduced some of the basics of cognitive psychology by helping you understand that cognitive psychology involves looking at cognitions assuming an information-processing approach. It also emphasised the notion that this needs to be done in a scientific way, and so to understand truly how to think like a cognitive psychologist you will need first to understand more about this.

The *scientific method* means that you need to test a hypothesis to examine variables that influence behaviour. Thus the hypothesis states that two variables are related in some way and altering one of them may cause the participant to alter the other. In psychology we are trying to show that our results are significant and due to the thing we have changed (called the independent variable) rather than due to chance.

In order to think like a cognitive psychologist you therefore need clearly to understand what a hypothesis is and what the role of variables are.

> *A hypothesis should be a precise, testable statement of a relationship between two or more variables.*

There are two types of variables that should be included in each hypothesis. An *independent variable* (IV) is the thing that the researcher **deliberately manipulates**, so it is the thing that she purposely changes. A *dependent variable* (DV) is what one hopes will alter as a result of what is **changed** (so the DV measures any changes the IV has produced).

Generally, one variable (the IV) is altered to see what effect it has on another variable (the DV). This means that *cause* and *effect* are being measured.

> *The IV is the thing you are changing.*
> *The DV is the thing you are measuring.*

You also need to be aware that your hypothesis can be tested using both experimental and non-experimental methods.

The principle difference is that experiments involve looking at whether manipulating one variable (the IV) has an effect on what you are measuring (the DV) and can involve laboratory experiments or field experiments. For example, In the laboratory the researcher deliberately manipulates variables using standardised procedures (the same method each time), whereas in a field experiment the researcher also deliberately manipulates the IV but does so in the participant's own natural environment.

In contrast, non-experimental methods may be more viable within the social context since, often, studying behaviour in the real world becomes unnatural if transferred to the laboratory and therefore a range of other methods may be required including:

- **Case studies**, which focus on one individual and their behaviour, thoughts, feelings and experiences.
- **Correlation**, which measures the strength of the relationship between two variables; for example, it tests if there is a relationship between two things. It does *not*, however, test cause and effect – so it does not say that one thing causes the other, but simply says there is some relationship between two things.
- **Questionnaires**, which use fixed and/or open-ended questions to make a quick and efficient assessment of people's attitudes.
- **Observations**, which look at the behaviour of participants in various situations and see 'a relatively unconstrained segment of a person's freely chosen behaviour as it occurs' (Coolican, 1990, p. 60). These can be structured or unstructured, but can be carried out in the participant's natural environment.

Such work also needs to be carried out according to ethical guidelines and special note needs to be made of those concerning deception, informed consent, withdrawal, debriefing and protection of participants from harm.

Once you understand what cognitive psychology is and how it can be investigated, you are halfway to understanding the key principles that underpin this module.

So how do you think like a cognitive psychologist?

You need to focus on how cognitions operate within the information-processing approach. You must consider how an individual processes information and what factors affect such processing. It is not a discipline that looks at how you behave/process information in a collective way (as a group, such as 'students'), but instead takes an individual slant.

To be a successful cognitive psychologist you will need to learn how to consider the theories presented as a scientist, that is, to talk about cognitive processes in the context of the research studies/theories. You will also need to be aware that cognitive psychologists use scientific methods when studying people and their cognitions, and that they can test their hypotheses in an experimental or non-experimental way provided that ethical guidelines are always met.

Furthermore, you not only need to understand what cognitive psychology actually is and how to research it, but also require a knowledge of psychology's wider theoretical perspectives. Each of the following therefore influences the way you might think about this field.

Cognitive theories apply even in social situations, for example, the central idea that people use their memory, perception, attention and other means of information processing to interpret and process information about the social situation and others around them. However, critical to this is also the idea that people are not passive in the social situation and are affected by group processes and theories proposed by social psychologists.

Cognitions proceed through appropriate developmental stages and therefore a knowledge of these aids an understanding of how cognitions are formed and develop.

When studying any topic in cognitive psychology, you need to be aware of how the above theories have influenced thinking on the subject, as this will help you understand their perspective/explanation of behaviour.

You must also consider the methodology and the advantages/disadvantages of the methods used, as this will help you evaluate their work.

1.6

learning outcomes and assessment

Learning Outcomes

At the end of your cognitive psychology module you should be able to:

- understand and describe the major theories and areas of research in cognitive psychology;
- think critically about the key studies/theories;
- understand and be able to evaluate the methods used to research cognitive psychology;
- relate the theories and thinking of cognitive psychologists to contemporary cognitive science;
- understand the basic history and development of cognitive psychology; and
- understand the relationship between cognitive psychology and other psychological approaches.

Assessment

You will be assessed in a number of ways, including essay writing, projects and discussion work. Put simply, there are two basic skills that you need to be a good psychologist, and it is these that your examiners will look for when assessing you:

- Your **knowledge and understanding** of psychological theories, concepts and studies: to demonstrate this you might give a definition of a psychological term, outline a theory or a particular study carried out.
- Your **evaluation** of a psychological theory/argument/study: this essentially requires you to say what is good or bad about a theory/argument/study and focuses on *how* a theory or idea can be supported by research and *how* it can be criticised by research.

If you simply write out the relevant study and state that it does support/criticise a theory, you will not gain marks. Your essay questions test more than your ability to memorise and rewrite information. Rather, you are expected to show that you have considered both sides of an argument and are able to draw an overall conclusion – you therefore explicitly need to show *how* a piece of evidence supports or criticises a theory/idea. It is the 'why' that will gain you the higher marks, on both this particular question and the paper generally. Put bluntly, this skill demonstrated in your answer is the single factor that will make a difference to achieving the lower or higher grades in your psychology degree.

With regard to achieving the degree you are aiming for, the following broad criteria should apply:

- **70+ marks will give you a first class honours degree** whereby you show a clear, coherent and logical argument that (most importantly) shows an excellent demonstration of the key arguments, concepts and studies and an ability critically to evaluate these. Such analysis needs to reflect original thought, must be related to the set question and must be well supported by scientific evidence gained by the application of your wider reading.
- **60–69 marks will give you an upper second class honours degree** and will require that you show a clear, coherent and logical argument with good performance in the areas above. The main difference here is that you display less originality of thought than of that required for a first class honours. So you will show a good grasp of concepts, the relationship between them, and support your arguments accordingly with the application of wider reading.
- **50–59 marks will give you a lower second class degree**, which means that you demonstrate an organised argument but one that has irrelevant material or omissions, with a general grasp of concepts and logical argument shown.

Content may not be directly related to the question and evaluations do not reflect original analysis. There is less evidence of wider reading.

- **40–49 marks would result in a third class degree**, whereby you show a basic understanding of the main concepts and arguments in cognitive psychology but there are errors or omissions and debate may be unstructured and irrelevant. There would also be little evidence of original thought, little use of scientific evidence to support arguments and little evidence of wider reading.

As you can see from these criteria, some of the key skills you require in psychology are an important feature of this text. However, remember that this book is not a replacement for the wider reading you need to gain top marks – it will simply supplement what you know.

1.7	
running themes	

There will be a number of common themes that will run throughout this book – no matter what topic you are studying, these 'running themes' will recur and it is important that you bear these in mind, mention them when appropriate and think about how they make an impact on the topic you are studying:

- ***Bottom-up processing***: processes influenced by environmental stimuli.
- ***Chunking:*** knowledge made up of smaller pieces of information.
- ***Cognitive neuropsychology***: normal human cognitions can be understood by looking at impaired functioning in brain damaged patients.
- ***Cognitive neuroscience***: techniques used to study brain functioning.
- ***Ecological validity***: the extent to which laboratory studies can be applied to the real world.
- ***Experimental cognitive psychology***: carries out experiments in the laboratory on normal people.
- ***Gestalt psychology***: based on the idea that cognitions involve active, rather than passive, processing of information.
- ***Innate:*** ability is inborn and genetically determined.
- ***Modularity***: the idea that cognitive systems have independent processes or modules.

- *Rehearsal*: processing involves the repetition of material that has already been analysed.
- *Schema*: a building block of knowledge about people, events and the world that is stored in long-term memory.
- *Semantics*: links between meaningful concepts.
- *Top-down processing*: processing based on experience and expectations.

These running themes will help you when using your textbooks as they underpin most topics in the syllabus and will help you to understand that there is common ground between these topics. When revising material, these themes will also provide you with a way of linking your ideas together and in building up a picture of how cognitive psychology applies to the real world. As you will see throughout this book such themes can be involved in a whole range of processes, for example, in attention and memory to name just two. At the start of each chapter the themes most important to the topic are listed, and in some cases expanded upon, to give you some indication of the lines along which you could develop your thinking in relation to the material you will gain from your texts and indeed the chapters themselves. Expanding upon these when writing your essays will ensure that you engage on a level of critical thinking that is vital if you want to gain the higher marks.

part two

course companion to the curriculum

2.1

visual processing/perception

Core Areas

- Accommodation
- Aerial perspective
- Affordances
- Binocular cues
- Convergence
- Cyclic theory
- Differentiation theory
- Direct theory of perception
- Enrichment theory
- Familiar size
- Indirect theory of perception
- Interposition
- Law of Pragnanz
- Linear perspective
- Location constancy
- Monocular cues
- Motion parallax
- Nature–nurture debate
- Neurophysiology
- Oculomotor cues
- Opponent process theory
- Optic array
- Optic flow
- Perceptual development
- Perceptual organisation
- Perceptual set
- Resonance

- Shading
- Shape constancy
- Size constancy
- Stereopsis
- Texture gradients
- Trichromatic theory
- Visual cliff
- Visual illusions
- Visual preference technique

Learning Outcomes

By the end of this chapter you should be able to:

- define and understand what is meant by each of the key terms outlined above;
- understand that perception is a diverse topic that has a physiological basis and which focuses on the nature–nurture debate and its development and, organisation, as well as on theories of general and colour perception; and
- be able to provide support for these areas using practical examples of perception, for example, illusions, constancies, depth cues and so on.

Running Themes

- Bottom-up processing
- Cognitive neuroscience
- Ecological validity
- Experimental cognitive psychology
- Gestalt psychology
- Innate
- Schema
- Semantics
- Top-down processing

Introduction

Hill (2001) believes that perception involves detecting a feature or object, perceiving depth and recognising patterns or objects.

The nature–nurture debate is an important one in perception and there is evidence for both views as seen throughout this chapter. Essentially, developmental theories argue that perception is an innate ability whilst perceptual adaptation and readjustment studies suggest it is a result of learning. For example, animal studies, such as that by Blakemore & Cooper (1970), indicated that kittens exposed only to vertical and horizontal lines in their environment only developed and responded to physiological pathways resembling this perceptual orientation.

Obviously, caution must be applied when transferring such an assumption to humans, although research into adaptation shows some evidence for both a mixture of learning and inborn ability. Cataract patients provide particularly good insight into this.

Neurophysiology of Perception

The eye

Light waves proceed from the cornea to the iris, with the pupil governing the amount of light that enters. The lens goes through a process of accommodation so that images can be projected onto the retina, which contains five layers of cells (photoreceptors, horizontal cells, bipolar cells, amacrine cells and retinal ganglion cells).

Eye-cortex

Information passes from the retina, through the lateral geniculate nuclei of the thalamus, to the (visual or striate) cortex. Here the parvocellular pathway assists the perception of colour and fine detail whilst the magnocellular pathway perceives movement. The optic nerve of each eye aids the perceptual process, as signals can proceed from these to the optic tract and optic chiasms and onto the lateral geniculate nuclei of the thalamus as above.

Various methods have been used to study perceptual development including behavioural, preference (how long attention is focused on objects) and habituation (measuring how long attention is paid to an object). Others include the measurement of eye movements and further physiological methods.

Perceptual Organisation

Perception can be organised in a number of ways. Gestalt theory of perceptual organisation is outlined below.

An important distinction in the area of depth perception is that between monocular cues requiring the use of one eye and binocular cues requiring both. Oculomotor cues are those that use the muscles around both eyes.

The ways in which these cues account for perceptual organisation are as follows.

Monocular cues

- **Aerial perspective**: distant objects lose contrast because light is dispersed as it travels through the atmosphere.
- **Familiar size**: previous experience about object size can be used to judge distance.
- **Interposition**: an object that is near hinders perception of another object because it essentially hides the other object from view.
- **Linear perspective**: parallel lines pointing away are perceived to be closer together when viewed in the distance.
- **Motion parallax**: images that are nearer appear to be going faster than those that are further away.
- **Shading**: helps depth perception, as it only occurs with 3-D objects.
- **Texture**: objects that slant away have a texture gradient that increases as you look at them from front to back.

Binocular/oculomotor cues

- **Accommodation**: depth perception results from the thickening of the lens when looking at close objects.
- **Convergence**: depth is perceived because when an object is close the eyes turn inwards to focus on it.
- **Stereopsis**: refers to the way in which depth is perceived when images are projected onto the retina of both eyes.

Bruno & Cutting (1988) believe, however, that depth cues are combined by either adding them together, selecting the most relevant one, or using them simultaneously.

Key Thinkers/Theories

Perceptual development

Fantz's visual preference task (1961)

Young infants (4 days–5 months old) were shown discs that either were blank or had features that resembled those of the human face in the correct position or jumbled up and showed a preference for the discs that most closely resembled the face. Fantz believed this supported the view that perception was innate and that a basic level of preference for social stimuli was developed even at this age.

Gibson & Walk's visual cliff experiment (1960)

A 'visual cliff', which was actually a table top, was designed whereby a check pattern was placed under one side (shallow end) and on the floor beneath the top on the other (deep end). Results found that babies (6½ –12 months old) were reluctant to crawl onto the deep side, thus supporting the idea that depth cues are innate because they are developed even at this age.

Piaget's enrichment theory

Infants usually develop their sensory and motor abilities in the sensori-motor stage before the age of two and their subsequent interaction with the world aids the development of innate schemas. After this, they are able to form new schemas through the process of accommodation. Perception therefore occurs because it is influenced by the expectations that result from such schemas.

Differentiation theory

Perception develops once distinctive features of objects can be transferred across situations and once they can be differentiated from irrelevant stimuli. Such differentiation tends to occur as a product of age.

Perceptual organisation

Gestalt theory–law of Pragnanz

Gestalt theory looks at how parts of an object that are separated belong together as a whole. Its most fundamental belief is the law of Pragnanz, which states that organisation 'will always be as "good" as the prevailing conditions allow' (Koffka, 1935, p. 110). It also gives other examples of how perception is organised including:

- **Law of proximity**: parts of an object that are close to each other will be grouped together and perceived as a whole.
- **Law of similarity**: patterns that are visually similar are grouped together.
- **Law of good continuation**: elements that are mostly uninterrupted are seen as continuous.
- **Law of closure**: missing parts are filled in to allow perception of the whole.
- **Apparent motion**: motion can be perceived even in the absence of movement, so a light that is flashing on and off is seen as moving because such movements are seen as one rather than two separate parts.

Colour perception

Young–Helmholtz's trichromatic theory

Found that three types of cone receptor account for colour perception, that is, receptors for blue, green and red. These are derived from the fact that each cone receptor has varying sensitivity; the first, to short-wave-length light; the second, to medium-; and the last, to long-wave-length, respectively, responding to each of the aforementioned colours. When combined, however, they can produce perception of any other colour.

Hering's opponent-process theory (1878)

Processing occurs because colour receptors are organised into two pairs – red–green and blue–yellow. When one is activated it prevents activation of the other.

Perception

Gibson's direct, bottom-up theory of perception (1950, 1966, 1979)

According to Gibson, perception is bottom-up (influenced by environmental stimuli) and direct. Perception results from sensation initially derived from the optic array, which picks up consistent information from the environment and does so even when there is interaction with different aspects of the environment (the consistency being referred to as invariants). Since this means that light is reaching the eye, it allows perception of depth, location and so on. Resonance aids the process whereby environmental stimuli are picked up and tuned into as an automatic process. Information thus takes the form of optic flow patterns (giving information on speed and direction of movement), texture gradients (closer objects seen in more detail than further ones) and affordances (detail about the function of objects).

Gregory's indirect, constructivist, top-down theory of processing (1972)

In contrast to the above theory, Gregory predicted that perception is an active process that is based on experience and expectations. Thus schemas (past knowledge, expectations and so on) make inferences about perceptual data. Perceptual constancies and illusions support this notion, that is, the size, shape and location of objects remain the same even when they are seen from different distances, angles and locations because the brain uses schemas to compensate for these changes and interprets on the basis of experience and expectations. A similar process occurs with illusions, of which there are numerous. To give just some examples, this process applies to distortions, ambiguous figures, paradoxical figures and fictions. Perceptual set is therefore also important. This is where previous experience, expectations, motivation and emotion create a bias towards the perception of particular stimuli (or aspects of them) whilst ignoring other available data.

Neisser's cyclic theory (1976)

Perception involves both bottom-up and top-down elements. It is simply the result of a cyclic (circular) process where previous learning/ schemas inform the information processing of perceptual stimuli, but when environmental stimuli fail to match such knowledge, then the schema has to be adapted so it is a constant process of adaptation.

REMEMBER

Perception

➢ It can be innate or based on cognitive developmental stages.
➢ It can be organised such that the whole is seen as greater than the sum of its parts.
➢ Types of cone and opponent-colour receptors allow for perception of colour.
➢ It can be the result of environmental stimuli or based on previous learning/experience.

Handy Hints for Evaluating the Work of Key Thinkers/Theories

- It is hard to generalise the results from Fantz's work, as it contained a very small sample size and one cannot be sure that the preference was due to the human resemblance rather than the overall symmetrical pattern.
- It is possible that failure to climb onto the deep side of Gibson & Walk's 'visual cliff' (1960) was a result of environmental learning/experience.
- It is hard to isolate the development of perception from other cognitive processes using Piaget's theory, because it was intended as a whole theory of cognitive development and to focus on just one aspect is inaccurate.
- Gestalt theory focuses too narrowly on perception of 2-D rather than 3-D patterns and is too simplistic, failing to account for complex stimuli or indeed just offering a description of perceptual organisation rather than providing any clear biological or psychological account of these processes.
- Theories of colour perception can be usefully applied to explain colour blindness since medium- or long-wavelength cones tend to be reduced, and thus the opponent processes of red–green are also involved.
- Gibson accounts well for the interaction between the environment and perception but he does not account for the complex nature of it, and his explanation of affordances and so on is far too simplistic and lacking in detail about the detection processes involved. He also fails to acknowledge the role of other cognitive processes, such as memory, in perception.
- Gregory's theory would predict errors in perception on the basis of experience but this is not reflected in practice.
- Neisser's theory provides an excellent account of how theories of perception can be combined but it does so rather too generally, and the exact interactive nature of bottom-up and top-down processes are unspecified.
- With all of these studies, consideration must be given to the applicability to laboratory research of the real-life use of perception.

Tasks

1 A number of Illusions can be used to support Gregory's theory of perception. These include Muller–Lyer illusions, the Ponzo illusion, The Necker Cube and the Kanizsa triangle. Draw a diagram to represent each of these. State whether they are distortions, ambiguous figures or fictions and then use Gregory's theory of perception to explain why they occur.

2 Outline research into culture differences in perception (no more than an A4 page).

3 Research studies into the effects of perceptual set. Thus, look up one study that shows how context influences perception, another, how past experience affects it and lastly, one each for motivation and emotion.

"Critically consider theories of visual perception"

This is a fairly straightforward question in many respects, as it simply asks for the bottom-up and top-down theories of perception. Initially you should therefore focus on outlining the principles behind each of these theories. Critically consider requires an extension beyond these skills, however, and requires that you provide relevant examples to support the theories, for instance, of the role of optic flow patterns, texture gradients and affordances for Gibson's theory and of illusions, constancies and perceptual set for Gregory's, thus integrating your research from the tasks above. Remember, on each occasion where you describe what these phenomena are, you will need to go on to specify exactly why perception is therefore either a result of the environmental stimuli or experience. Lastly, a section will be required to balance out this discussion and you will need to produce arguments against the theories presented, again expanding on why they pose difficulties, before reaching an overall conclusion.

"What do research studies tell us about the development of perception?"

Notice the focus here is on research studies. In any opening paragraph you may want to highlight the nature–nurture debate and its relevance to perceptual development. You then have opposing research studies to highlight the aspects of this debate. Fantz's study will need to be outlined in detail and then you need to go on to show what this research actually tells us about perceptual development, that is, it highlights that it is an innate skill. This can then be balanced out by Gibson & Walk's study on the visual cliff. Again, you will need to outline this before expanding on how it supports the idea that perception is a result of learning. Since neither study alone can solely account for each perspective, the notes of caution should be discussed, all the time referring back to what these points say about perceptual development.

Common Pitfalls

- *Undoubtedly this is an extensive topic with many difficult terms to grasp and students frequently mix these up. It may therefore be useful to draw up a list of definitions to revise at the start of this topic.*
- *When discussing the theories of perception, it is essential that you go beyond simply describing the theories and, more importantly, must use the evidence on constancies, illusions and so on to support them.*
- *When studying perceptual development ensure that you can relate the data back to a discussion on nature–nurture and therefore prepare, in advance, how each study supports a nature or nurture argument.*

Textbook guide

GREGORY R. L. (1997). *Eye and brain: The psychology of seeing (5th ed.).* Princeton, NJ: Princeton University Press. This gives a much more extensive coverage of the physiology behind vision.

BRUCE, V., GREEN, P. P., & GEORGESON, M. A. (1966). *Visual perception: Physiology, psychology and ecology.* Hove, UK: Psychology Press This provides a more detailed coverage of those topics involved in perception.

FANTZ, R. L. (1961). The origin of form perception. *Scientific American, 204,* 66–72. Original coverage of this important study.

GIBSON, E. J., & WALK, R. D. (1960). The visual cliff. *Scientific American, 202,* 64–71. Original coverage of this important study.

2.2	
object recognition	

Core Areas

- Cognitive demon
- Decision demon
- Face recognition
- Feature demon
- Feature detection theory
- Full primal sketch
- Geons
- Image demon
- Marr's computational model
- Normalisation
- Pandemonium model of feature detection
- Pattern recognition
- Prototype theory
- Range map
- Raw primal sketch

- Template theory
- 3-D representation
- 2.5-D representation

Learning Outcomes

By the end of this chapter you should be able to:

- define the key terms;
- distinguish between theories of pattern recognition and face recognition;
- understand the psychological explanations of object recognition and the contribution made by neuroscience;
- acknowledge the work of key thinkers in this area; and
- critically evaluate their work.

Running Themes

- Bottom-up processing
- Ecological validity
- Experimental cognitive psychology
- Gestalt psychology
- Modularity
- Top-down processing

Introduction

Eysenck & Keane (2000) outline the three key processes involved in object recognition; the fact that environmental stimuli overlap so a decision has to be made about the beginning and end of objects, they need to be recognised from different orientations and distances and categorisation must take place, which can involve the allocation of diverse stimuli to the same group of objects.

This topic involves looking at both pattern recognition and face recognition. Pattern recognition looks at the categorisation of 2-D patterns whilst face recognition focuses on the processes involved in recognising faces.

Theories of Pattern Recognition

Template theory

Argues that LTM contains templates of patterns which are matched to the visual input and involves various templates.

> Normalisation is an important part of the process whereby an internal representation about standard features of the template is produced before seeking a template.

Prototype theory

Proposes that there is a matching process which is very specific since only one prototype exists for a given category; thus a comparison takes place such that the pattern is either recognised or not, and if not it is then subsequently compared to another prototype.

Feature theory

Focuses on the idea that there are key features within patterns which are perceived and compared to information already held in memory. There is some discussion as to whether a detailed analysis leads to a general assumption, or vice versa. Visual search research supports these ideas, for example, identifying the target letter Z took less time if it was set amongst rounded rather than straight letters, because the rounded letters shared fewer common features so could be compared more rapidly (Neisser, 1964).

 **REMEMBER**

Theories of Pattern Recognition

Theories of pattern recognition involve:

➢ matching visual templates with those already held in LTM
➢ the matching of prototypes (or basic concepts)
➢ perceiving and comparing features of a stimulus with those already held in memory.

Handy Hints for Evaluating Theories of Pattern Recognition

- The biggest difficulty with template theory is that it would have to be assumed that all patterns require their own template, which is not feasible beyond the simplest of shapes or ones that cannot be easily classified as part of a given category.
- It is generally recognised, however, that there is some basis for the idea that pattern recognition involves a matching process, but the stage of processing at which this occurs is not clear-cut.
- Prototype theory accounts for the complexity of the above approach and instead proposes a much more economical explanation of processing such information, but does not address the common errors often made in recognising similar letters, nor the role of context.
- Feature theory also fails to account for contextual information and the role of expectations. It ignores the relationships between features. Furthermore, the application of findings from the laboratory to the real-life setting is questionable since things are not seen in isolation in the same way as laboratory testing sets up.

Key Thinkers

Selfridge's pandemonium model of feature detection (1959)

Four hierarchical stages are involved in processing features and this process occurs in parallel using an analogy of demons. Initially, an object is represented as an image, which is a biological process where it falls onto the retina (image demon), and features are then analysed and compared, for instance, for lines and angles (the feature demon). Subsequently, components are recognised and meaningful patterns constructed (cognitive demons) and lastly, patterns are recognised as a result of this matching process.

This is called the pandemonium model because of the supposed chaos caused by the demons shouting to each other!

Marr's computational theory (1982)

According to this model, individuals construct and then work through three hierarchical stages of representation before being able to recognise an object. An initial (retinal) representation (described by Marr as having two phases: 'the raw primal sketch', which recognises various light intensities; and 'the full primal sketch', which outlines shapes) provides basic information about the features of the object to form a 2.5-D sketch. At the second stage of representation, individuals interpret the 2.5-D from their own particular point of view. Finally, at the third stage, binocular disparity enables individuals to process more detailed information about the objects, for example, depth (using the range map) and orientation, and subsequently construct a 3-D model based on the simple construction of an image (accessibility), its scope and uniqueness, and the similarities shared by and differences between objects (stability and sensitivity) (Marr & Nishihara, 1978).

Biederman's recognition-by-components theory (1987)

Developed from Marr's work, this approach suggests that 36 basic shapes are recognised (geons) and pattern recognition occurs once the combination and spatial arrangement of these are identified. Identification of five 'invariant properties' is required, that is, more simply, if the edges are straight, converging, parallel, symmetrical or curving, these are then matched to the images/templates already held in memory. As part of this process, it means recognition can take place even if only part of the object can be viewed and when some information is not retrievable.

Because the components represent templates that are then matched to aid recognition, then it is aptly named the recognition-by-components theory.

Humphreys, Lanote & Lloyd-Jones's interactive activation and competition model (1995)

Structural descriptions of visually similar objects generate semantic and then name representations and each of these is connected.

Farah & McClelland's connectionist model (1991)

A number of systems are connected in this computational model: visual and verbal systems linked by a semantic system. Thus a visual representation is made and the name of the object is coded within the verbal system. Object recognition proceeds through a series of stages, from the visual, to the semantic and then the verbal system. Here, the semantic system is key, since it links visual characteristics to functions of objects. Thus all aspects are connected–hence the model's title.

Bruce & Young's face recognition (1986)

Eight components are involved in recognising faces: an initial description (structural encoding), analysis of expression, analysis of facial speech, selective processing of facial information (directed visual processing), constructing information about faces, identifying nodes about personal information, storing the person's name, and adding any other important information. As such, recognition of familiar and unfamiliar faces can take place. Eysenck & Keane (2000) suggest that recognition of familiar faces principally involves structural encoding, face recognition, personal information and naming, whilst recognition of unfamiliar faces involves encoding, expression and facial speech analysis, and direct visual processing.

REMEMBER

Theories of Object Recognition

➤ Objects are represented as images. Features are then analysed and compared (for instance, for lines and angles), components are recognised and meaningful patterns constructed; thus patterns are recognised as a result of this matching process.

➤ Three hierarchical stages of representation are constructed and then worked through. An initial (retinal) representation provides basic information about the features of the object to form a 2.5-D sketch. At the second stage of representation, the 2.5-D sketch is interpreted from an individual viewpoint. Finally, at the third stage, binocular disparity enables more detailed information about depth and orientation to be processed, and subsequently a 3-D model is constructed about the object.

➤ Thirty-six basic shapes are recognised (geons) and pattern recognition occurs once the combination and spatial arrangement of these are identified.

➤ Visual and verbal systems linked by a semantic system give meaning and lead to recognition.

Handy Hints for Evaluating the Work of Key Thinkers

• Context and the role of expectations have been ignored by Selfridge's model and spatial and angular distortions cannot be accounted for within a real-life context.

- As with all of these theories testing object recognition within a laboratory setting, it is hard to generalise the findings to a wider context.
- Marr's theory and that of Biederman still have some difficulty in accounting for how objects with unfamiliar parts are identified, although Biederman has successfully extended the basic concepts presented by Marr.
- It is difficult to empirically test the notion that there are 36 specific geons, and the assumption that information about edges is sufficient for object recognition is questionable.
- The connectionist model usefully applies to practice and explains why some patients with brain injuries are unable to recognise living objects, although the subdivision of the semantic system into visual and functional areas is hard to test precisely and may therefore be an inaccurate separation. It is also somewhat simplistic and processing of objects is probably more complex than this computer model suggests.

> There is also further evidence in the field of cognitive neuroscience, especially in the field of agnosia, that tells us something about the way in which object recognition normally works. Since many of the theories covered above involve a series of processing stages, brain damaged patients therefore have impaired recognition and there are numerous case studies to support this idea.

Tasks

1 As a practical exercise you could try to replicate the study carried out by Navon (1977). This involved giving participants a large letter made up of smaller letters and testing if it took longer to recognise the bigger letter when such letters correspond rather than contradict. Carry this out on a sample of your friends/tutorial group and then, using the psychological theories provided, discuss why such a result would be found.

2 Complete Table 1, Which requires you to extend your reading of this topic, and find at least one type of experimental support for each of the models of recognition outlined.

3 Face recognition is a much wider topic than has been possible to present here and it is imperative that you have a greater depth of understanding. To fully appreciate Bruce & Young's model (1986) you therefore need to use your textbooks and library resources to produce an A4 page detailing supporting work on one side and a list of criticisms on the other. It might also help your understanding to think about the techniques you yourself use to recognise people.

TABLE 1   Support For Theories of Object Recognition

Theory	Support	How Does this Support The Theory?
Marr's Computational theory (1982)		
Biederman's recognition-by-components theory (1987)		
Humphreys et al.'s interactive activation and competition model (1995)		
Farah & McClelland's connectionist model (1991)		

"Discuss explanations of pattern recognition"

Here you initially need to outline the explanations that psychologists have offered for pattern recognition. As a reminder, these include Selfridge's model (1959) whereby images of objects are represented as images, features are analysed and compared, components are recognised and meaningful patterns constructed, and patterns are recognised as a result of this matching process; Marr's Theory (1982) which states that three representations are formed and worked through; Biederman's theory (1987) where 36 basic shapes are recognised (geons) and pattern recognition occurs once the combination and spatial arrangement of these are identified; and Farah & McClelland's visual and verbal systems linked by a semantic system that gives meaning and leads to recognition (1991). This will, however, provide you with only an initial outline of the theories rather than the depth required by a discussion-based essay. You therefore need to be able to expand on the experimental support for these as derived from your research in the above task. Furthermore, these explanations of pattern recognition are not without their problems, for example, all of these theories test object recognition within a laboratory setting, so it is hard to generalise the findings to a wider context. Marr's theory and that of Biederman still have some difficulty in accounting for how objects with unfamiliar parts are identified; it is also difficult to empirically test Biederman's notion that there are 36 specific geons, and the assumption that information about edges is sufficient for object recognition is questionable. Also, the subdivision of the semantic system into visual and functional areas is hard to test precisely and may therefore be an inaccurate separation. Again this addresses points of relevance, but you will need to engage more fully with the material and tell the examiner exactly why each of these points poses problems for the given models. Only by doing so will the requirements for any discussion question be met.

"Outline and evaluate research into face recognition"

Inevitably Bruce and Young's model is going to be the focal point for this essay and the most critical part of the outline component to the question will be an explanation of this. However, the title specifically asks you to be aware of research into this area and thus the work you have completed for task 3 above will feed directly into this. In order to evaluate, you will need to specify how research studies support the model, for example, which parts/processes, and then consider the general difficulties that can be found with both the model itself and the research studies, including the applicability of research into face recognition in a real-life context. As a general tip, evaluating research can therefore also include analysis of the research methods used.

Common Pitfalls

- *Each area of object recognition is quite separate, for example, patterns versus objects versus faces, and sometimes students forget to make any distinction between these, which is important.*
- *As highlighted above, it is necessary to focus specifically on what the essay question asks, so a general discussion is quite different to being asked to outline and evaluate research. It is tempting to learn material in a general fashion and then write it all down regardless of the question, so remember your material must be tailored to what is required.*
- *If you are unsure about the role of bottom-up/top-down processing in each of the theories of object recognition, it would be useful to work through these before proceeding with any written work.*

Textbook guide

BIEDERMAN, I. (1987). Recognition-by-components: A theory of human image understanding. *Psychological Review, 94,* 115–247. Provides a much more extensive coverage of this important theory.

BRUCE, V., & HUMPHREYS, G. W. (1994). *Object and face recognition.* Hove: UK: Psychology Press. A text explicitly focused on this topic and therefore giving an in-depth discussion of the areas involved.

TURNBALL, O. H., BESCHIN, N., & DELLA-SALA, S. (1997). Agnosia for object orientation: Implications for theories of object recognition. *Neuropsychologia, 35,* 153–163. This outlines the relevance of neuropsychological evidence in much more detail than has been possible in this chapter and gives some interesting insight to the contribution such research makes into object recognition.

2.3

speech/word recognition

Core Areas

- Automatic processing
- Cohort theory
- Interactive activation model
- Motor theory
- Prosodic cues
- Response bias effect
- Semantic priming effects
- Sensitivity effect
- TRACE model

Learning Outcomes

By the end of this chapter you should be able to:

- define the key terms;
- provide an introductory outline to the processes involved in word recognition including phonemic restoration, lip reading, prosodic cues, automatic processing, the role of context and letter identification;
- understand the role of bottom-up and top-down processes in relation to explanation of recognition including motor theory, cohort theory, the TRACE model and the interactive activation model; and
- consider the strengths and weaknesses of each of these theories in explaining speech/word recognition.

Running Themes

- Bottom-up processing
- Ecological validity

- Experimental cognitive psychology
- Schema
- Semantics
- Top-down processing

Introduction

Recognising words may be due to data-driven processes resulting from things we hear (bottom-up processing) or from the concepts taken from linguistic context (top-down processing). The latter, partially deriving from the phonemic restoration effect whereby context is used to fill in (hence restore) parts of a missing sentence, occurs because of sensitivity and response bias effects. In other words, it happens because of the signals that are heard and the additional information provided about context.

Prosodic cues also help word recognition (that is, cues such as stress placed on a word, intonation, etc.), and lip reading has been found to play a role.

Word identification may further involve the following processes:

Automatic processing

Where a word is processed unavoidably without much conscious aware-ness. The Stroop effect is an excellent indicator of this.

Semantic priming effect

When sentences contain words that add meaning or context, then recognition is faster, probably because such priming leads to the activation of related words stored within memory and because this occurs after lexical processing.

Letter identification

It was originally assumed that individual letters require recognition as a prerequisite to recognising words; however, contradictory thought suggests that words have superiority over letters and actually aid letter recognition rather than vice versa.

> Word recognition can be a fairly automatic process that involves different processes including filling in missing sounds, using non-verbal cues and lip reading, using context and identifying letters.

Key Thinkers

Liberman et al's motor theory (1967)

Listeners copy the speech/motor movements made by the speaker and so can recognise words even when the context may be ambiguous.

Marslen-Wilson & Tyler's cohort theory (1980)

A word initial cohort is derived from sounds which then activate recognised words that have been presented auditorally. If they do not match the presented information or relate to the context or meaning of the word, then they are eliminated and the recognition point simply occurs when this matching processing is complete and all other possibilities have indeed been eliminated. Thus there is an interaction and combination of all language aspects such as meaning, grammar, etc. before word recognition takes place. Word monitoring tasks support the idea that parallel processing occurs in speech recognition and depends upon both the data presented (bottom-up processing) and the concepts derived from linguistic context (top-down processing). A revision of the theory (Marslen-Wilson, 1990; Marslen-Wilson & Warren, 1994) suggested a more flexible approach, where the initial cohort was less stringently selective than had been proposed originally and instead incorporated any word with similar initial sounds, with the role of context having less of an impact and occurring later on in processing.

TRACE model, McClelland & Elman (1986), McClelland (1991)

Like the above theory, there is an interaction of many features of language but most importantly that data-driven processes resulting from things we hear (bottom-up processing) interact with the concepts taken from linguistic context (top-down processing). Units containing the features of speech, the sounds and words are connected progressively (so features to sounds, sounds to words in bottom-up processing and vice versa for top-down processing). The interaction between these levels is, however, dependent on their activation, where a trace is formed based on the spreading of information between such units, whilst subject to excitation and inhibitory processes.

McClelland & Rumelhart's interactive activation model (1981)

Again, both bottom-up and top-down processing are involved in word recognition, although evidence for this theory was largely based purely on the recognition of four letter words. Once more, three levels are involved:

the feature level, letter level (identifying letter positioning within a word) and the recognising of the actual word. Bottom-up processing therefore operates from feature to word via letter whilst the opposite is true for top-down processing. It works such that any words containing similar features or letters are activated whilst all other possibilities are inhibited, so that one word is left to be recognised. Later developments of the model tried to account for the speed as well as accuracy of recognition.

The key feature that most of these approaches share is the combined role of bottom-up and top-down processing in word recognition, or put more simply both the data presented (bottom-up processing) and the concepts derived from linguistic context (top-down processing).

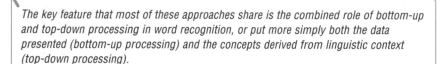

REMEMBER

Theories of Word Recognition

➤ Listeners copy the speech/motor movements made by the speaker and so can recognise words even when the context may be ambiguous.

➤ *A word initial cohort is derived from sounds which then activate recognised words. If they do not match the presented information or relate to the context or meaning of the word, then they are eliminated and the recognition point simply occurs when this matching processing is complete and all other possibilities have indeed been eliminated.*

➤ *Units containing the features of speech, the sounds and words are connected progressively (so features to sounds, sounds to words in bottom-up processing and vice versa for top-down processing) and words are recognised subject to activation and inhibitory processes.*

➤ *Words containing similar features or letters are activated whilst all other possibilities are inhibited, so that one word is left to be recognised.*

Handy Hints for Evaluating the Work of Key Thinkers

• Motor theory can be contradicted by the real-life evidence that is seen in word recognition of young children who have little experience of motor production in their early years but are nonetheless very astute at recognising words; therefore word recognition must be more complex than the theory would suggest.

- The development of cohort theory was widely accepted as being a more useful version, especially with regard to the greater degree of flexibility it offered and the stage of contextual processing it presented, although with the flexibility comes less precise specification about its exact operation.
- The TRACE model incorrectly assumed that activation is an immediate response to phonological similarities and there was an overemphasis on the importance of contextual and semantic information. The interactive nature of processing is also questionable and the model cannot account for individual differences in speech patterns such as timing and speech rates. As with many models focused on language, there is difficulty in generalising the information and results obtained from computer simulations to speech within the real-life context, and as such the theory lacks ecological validity.

Tasks

1 Using Figure 1, draw arrows to represent the interaction between the three levels involved in the interactive activation model and underneath the figure describe what it shows.

2 Fill in Worksheet 1 on theories of word recognition.

3 Fold an A4 piece of paper in half, and half again, giving you four squares. Then put in the headings 'motor theory', 'cohort theory', 'TRACE model', 'interactive activation model'. Under each of these record the role of first, bottom-up processing and, second, top-down processing. If you can't remember the definition of each of these, then look them up again and write them clearly on this paper so that you can refer to them.

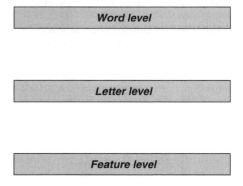

Figure 1 The Interactive Activation Model

"Discuss the extent to which psychological theories explain word recognition"

This question involves two main skills. Firstly, it requires you to show that you know something about psychological theories of word recognition and therefore you will need to provide a description of the range of possible theories. As this is only one component of the essay, however, you do not need to spend pages and pages outlining them since this would not directly tackle the set question. In order to address the issue 'to what extent do they explain recognition?' the other skill you will need to show is your ability to evaluate each theory. In other words, telling your examiner the strengths and weaknesses of the theories and elaborating on why they are strengths and weaknesses. Only by doing this will you be able to draw any overall conclusions on how well word recognition can be explained by psychological theory. In order to ensure that you keep on track, it would be most helpful to refer back to the theory you have just discussed and directly answer the extent to which it explains recognition, rather than making sweeping, generalised statements at the end of the overall discussion.

"Examine the role of bottom-up and top-down processes in word/speech recognition"

Task 3 above is specifically designed to help you plan for this essay. It requires not only a general understanding of the theories themselves, but also a specific understanding of how bottom-up and top down processes relate to these theories. For example, both cohort theory and the TRACE model support the idea that parallel processing occurs in speech recognition and depends upon both the data presented (bottom-up processing) and the concepts derived from linguistic context (top-down processing). In the interactive activation model, bottom-up processing operates from feature to word via letter, whilst the opposite is true for top-down processing. These issues can be used as a starting point for discussion and then an outline of the theory to make this link more explicit can follow. Any criticisms of the exact contribution made by such processes can then be made before an overall summary is made.

Common Pitfalls

- *Understanding this topic requires at least a basic understanding of the key terms involved in language, for example, lexicons, semantics and so on. Too often, students fail to understand these and try learning the theories of word recognition by rote, hoping a lack of understanding will not be apparent. Unfortunately, however, they are crucial in truly grasping the finer points and you therefore need to ensure some familiarity with them.*
- *Since the role of bottom-up and top down processing is fundamental to most of the theories in this topic, you need to understand the contribution they make.*
- *Sometimes you may be tempted to simply look at the key words in the title and write down everything you know about word recognition without focusing directly on what the question is asking. Look at the titles above to help you identify a format to avoid this.*

Textbook guide

CARREIRAS, M., & GRAINGER, J. (2004). *Sublexical representations in visual word recognition.* Hove, UK: Psychology Press. This describes the functional units that intervene between low-level perceptual processes and access to whole word representation in LTM during visual word recognition. It presents evidence in favour of more flexible coding schemes than is typical.

MARSLEN-WILSON, W. D., & WARREN, P (1994). Levels of perceptual representation and process in lexical access: Words, phonemes and features. *Psychological Review, 101,* 653–675. A more detailed account than this chapter gives on the revised cohort model.

WORKSHEET 1 THEORIES OF WORD RECOGNITION

Match the following theories of word recognition to their description and criticisms using arrows to link each one

The interactive nature of processing is also questionable and the model cannot account for individual differences in speech patterns such as timing and speech rates.

Listeners copy the speech/motor movements made by the speaker and so can recognise words even when the context may be ambiguous.

TRACE model

Words containing similar features or letters are activated whilst all other possibilities are inhibited, so that one word is left to be recognised.

Motor theory

Young children have little experience of motor production in their early years but are nonetheless very astute at recognising words; therefore word recognition must be more complex than the theory would suggest.

There is not enough precise specification about its exact operation.

It incorrectly assumed that activation is an immediate response to phonological

similarities and there 'was an overemphasis on...' the importance of contextual and semantic information.

A word initial cohort is derived from sounds which then activate recognised words. If they do not match the presented information or relate to the context or meaning of the word, then they are eliminated and the recognition point simply occurs when this matching processing is complete and all other possibilities have indeed been eliminated.

As with many models focused on language, there is difficulty in generalising the information and results obtained from computer simulations to speech within the real-life context, and as such the theory lacks ecological validity.

Units containing the features of speech, the sounds and words are connected progressively (so features to sounds, sounds to words in bottom-up processing and vice versa for top-down processing) and words are recognised subject to activation and inhibitory processes.

Cohort theory

2.4	
attention	

Core Areas

- Attentional engagement theory
- Attenuator theory
- Automatic processing
- Bottleneck theory
- Central capacity theory
- Controlled processing
- Divided attention
- Feature integration theory
- Filter theory
- Focused/selective attention
- Guided search theory
- Late selection theory
- Modular theory
- Spotlight theory
- Synthesis theory
- Zoom theory

Learning Outcomes

By the end of this chapter you should be able to:

- define the key terms outlined above;
- understand that there are different types of attention (focused/selective and divided);
- describe and evaluate theories of focused attention including filter, attenuator and late selection theories and that of Johnston & Heinz (1978).
- outline theories of visual attention such as spotlight, zoom, feature integration, guided search and attentional engagement; and

- discuss research into divided attention, such as bottleneck and central capacity theories and modular and synthesis explanations.

Running Themes

- Ecological validity
- Experimental cognitive psychology
- Modularity
- Rehearsal
- Semantics

Introduction

Attention is 'the focusing and concentration of mental effort that usually results in conscious awareness of certain aspects of external sensory stimuli or mental experiences' (Hill, 2001,p.113).

There are two types of attention:

1 **Focused/selective attention:** concentrates on how attention is focused on particular input stimulus, why it is selective and what happens to the non-attended stimuli.

2 **Divided attention:** looks at how attention can be devoted to more than one input stimulus and what the capacities are on this.

Eysenck & Keane (2000) believe that attention is affected by:

- **Task difficulty:** as it is harder to perform two different tasks.
- **Practice:** if one (or both) tasks are well practised then they are easier to perform.
- **Similarity:** similar tasks are harder to perform simultaneously due to interference, which is most common when they use the same modality, processing stage or response mechanism.

Related to this topic (although beyond the scope of covering fully in this chapter) is the idea of *automatic processing,* which occurs when tasks are practised and therefore require less attention, so it is easier to perform them simultaneously. Eysenck & Keane (2000, p. 141) state that automatic processes are ones that are fast, demand little attention/don't reduce capacity for performance, are unavailable to consciousness and are unavoidable.

Schneider & Shiffrin (1977) distinguished between:

- *controlled processing*, which is slow, makes heavy demands, has a limited capacity but encourages flexible processing, and requires direct attention; and
- *Automatic processing*, which is unavoidable, parallel, doesn't require attention, and is unaffected by capacity.

Most research into this area looks at attention in relation to external, rather than internal, processes because they are easier to control and measure.

REMEMBER

Theories of Attention

➢ *Selective theories:* look at how attention is selective and focused on just one input.

➢ *Divided theories:* look at the division of attention between two stimuli.

➢ *Automatic processing:* looks at the automaticity of processing and whether it is controlled or automatic, with each requiring different levels of attention.

Key Thinkers in Focused/Selective Attention

Cherry (1953)

Used the 'cocktail party situation' because he was interested in how we focus on just one conversation in a room full of others. He used two types of tests to research this. *Binaural tests* – when two different messages were presented to both ears simultaneously he found no differences in distinguishing between them if they were presented in the same voice and intensity, but if there were physical differences (for example, gender of presenter), then it affected attention. *Dichotic tests* – when a different message was presented to each ear and participants were asked to repeat just one, the non-attended message was retained according to physical differences but not semantics.

Broadbent's filter theory (1958)

Assumptions of this theory are that two similar stimuli gain parallel access to a sensory register that briefly holds the information; a selective filter then allows one input through on the basis of physical characteristics and the other channel rests in the buffer. This is followed by some limited capacity processing and an output response. The importance of the filter, therefore, is that it prevents overload.

Treisman's attenuation theory (1960)

Assumes that the non-attended input is not rejected but is 'attenuated' (diminished) compared to attended information. All attenuated channels are then analysed semantically (that is, information is selected for its meaning) and information that has either personal important or current relevance is recognised thus making an output response therefore possible.

Deutsch & Deutsch's late selection theory (1963)

Assumes that all input is analysed equally for meaning and the filter occurs as a result of a late selection process. Selection will again be based on relevance of the input.

Johnston & Heinz (1978)

Proposed that there is actually a flexible model where the more stages of processing before selection results in more demands being placed on processing capacity. Selection therefore occurs as early on as possible to minimise these demands. This was supported by Johnston & Wilson (1980), who found that selection can be made at any stage depending on the situational demands.

Handy Hints for Evaluating The Work of Key Thinkers in Focused/Selective Attention

- Broadbent's theory is seen as being too inflexible and doesn't account for analysis of the non-shadowed message.
- It is possible that the non-attended message is dealt with and processed without awareness, and this was not accounted for by Broadbent's theory.

- It is possible that attention can be switched between channels more easily than Broadbent believed possible.
- Some argue that Broadbent incorrectly assumed that the unattended message is rejected at an early stage of processing, but this may be a result of the method of testing rather than attentional processes.
- Treisman's own work can be supported by his finding that words from a non-attended sentence would be added to the attended sentence if it made it meaningful.
- Gray & Wedderburn (1960) supported Treisman because if given two different sentences 'what ...6 ...hell' and '2 ...the ...9', then participants could report them as whole meaningful sentences, showing that there was analysis of meaning for both messages and this was switched between channels.
- However, Tresiman's theory is complex and the exact role of the attenuator is questionable.
- Deutsch & Deutsch's theory has not been supported by experimental evidence. For example, Treisman & Riley (1969) found that target words were better detected in shadowed compared to non-shadowed messages, as this cannot be explained by a process where there is supposed to be equal semantic analysis.

REMEMBER

Theories of Selective Attention

> *Filter theory:* stimuli gain parallel access to a sensory register that briefly holds the information, then a selective filter allows one input through on the basis of physical characteristics.

> *Attenuator theory:* the non-attended input is 'attenuated' (diminished) then analysed semantically.

> *Late selection theory:* all input is analysed equally for meaning and the filter occurs as a result of a late selection process.

> *Johnston & Heinz's theory:* the more stages of processing before selection results in more demands placed on processing capacity. Selection therefore occurs as early on as possible to minimise these demands

Theories of Focused Visual Attention

Spotlight theory

Resembles the idea that we have a small field of vision and it is hard to see things outside of this spotlight region, although attention can be shifted by moving this light.

Zoom theories

Eriksen & St James (1986) instead proposed that attention is more like a zoom lens which can be adjusted to cover a large area in much detail or a small area in specific detail, so the size of visual field that is attended to can vary.

Treisman's – feature integration theory (1988/1992)

There is a distinction between objects and their features (for example, colour) where all basic features are processed rapidly, in parallel and in an automatic, pre-attentive way. Features are combined in a serial process – to form objects – which is influenced by knowledge, but in the absence of knowledge, illusions may be created.

Wolfe's – guided search theory (1998)

This is similar to the above as there is an initial feature base, then subsequent general search process. It is not, however, assumed that processing is parallel then serial. Instead, initial feature processing produces an activation map, with each input showing individual levels; attention is then allocated on the basis of highest–lowest activation.

Duncan & Humphrey's – attentional engagement theory (1989, 1992)

All items are analysed in terms of their features and then a later stage of processing occurs where input is matched for its likeness in STM. Here, speed is determined by the amount of desegregation required and the similarity present in non-target items; thus items that are similar will be selected together.

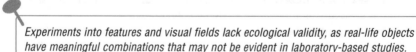

Experiments into features and visual fields lack ecological validity, as real-life objects have meaningful combinations that may not be evident in laboratory-based studies.

Key Thinkers in/Theories of Divided Attention

Bottleneck theories

A bottleneck makes it harder for two descriptions to be made similar. This is supported by the psychological refractory period, which is the delay caused by the increased information processing time when a second stimulus closely follows the first.

Kahneman's central capacity theory (1973)

This model is seen as being more flexible, with one central processor responsible for allocating attention. Attention is therefore a skill more than a simple process. Capacity is limited but varies. Most attention will be devoted to tasks where there is a high level of difficulty. The capacity available is dependent upon arousal level and attention is allocated according to the effort required, current goals/ objectives and importance.

Allport's modular theory (1989)

Proposes that attention consists of several specific information processing modules, each with its own resources and capacities. Similar tasks interfere if they therefore use the same module's resources, but in parallel processing it can occur if they are dissimilar, as interference is not created.

Baddeley's synthesis theory (1986)

Based on the idea of the working memory model (WMM) – modality free, central, limited capacity processing and therefore modality processing systems.

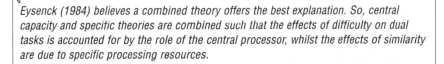

Eysenck (1984) believes a combined theory offers the best explanation. So, central capacity and specific theories are combined such that the effects of difficulty on dual tasks is accounted for by the role of the central processor, whilst the effects of similarity are due to specific processing resources.

Handy Hints for Evaluating Theories of Divided Attention

- Since theories rely on the findings of task difficulty, it is important to note that this is too easily confused with similarity in experimental tasks to be of real use.
- Capacity is unspecified in Kahneman's theory and modular theorists would disagree that processing resources are general and undifferentiated.
- On the other hand, modular theories need more specification, for example, the number and type of modules and their exact nature of interaction.

Tasks

1 Draw a flow chart or spider diagram summarising the different theories of attention and put the heading 'focused attention' on one page and 'divided attention' on the other. Now fill in the appropriate theories/subheadings for each one.

2 Use your textbooks to research supporting and criticising evidence for theories of focused visual attention.

3 Fill in Table 2 on theories of focused attention.

"Describe and evaluate research (theories and/or studies) of focused/selective attention"

There are many theories of selective attention as outlined above and it is unlikely that in any timed/examination essay it will be possible to cover all of them. The danger of attempting this is that you end up describing each one without considering the merits or disadvantages of the explanations offered or techniques used. The essay should start with a broad description of focused attention followed by an outline/definition of the specific theories you wish to focus on. Both this and your outline of the appropriate research will give you your description marks. Note, however, that the question also asks you to evaluate the research and this involves more than simply listing points/studies of relevance. In order to gain the higher marks, it requires that you really engage in the material and elaborate on exactly why each strength and weakness contributes or detracts from the theory or why each study supports or criticises. Remember it is also important to consider the research methods used, especially the issue of ecological validity.

"Assess the insight that research has given to us about the nature of divided attention"

Essentially this essay asks you to consider each of the theories presented in this topic. By asking you about the nature of divided attention it is asking you to outline the theories and their supporting evidence and use this to explain what this tells us. For example, how is attention divided and what factors affect this? You need to be clear about the support given, as it is this that provides the insight; merely describing the theory does not reflect this and will alternatively show the examiners that you are rewriting material from your textbook with little understanding. In order to achieve a balanced argument, however, you also need to discuss the weaknesses of these theories, or the methods in which they were tested, because it may be that they do provide valuable insight into the nature of divided attention but in the context of some limitations or points that need to be considered before fully accepting their usefulness.

Common Pitfalls

- *This is an extensive topic even without the additional reading required on automatic processing and action slips, which was beyond the scope of this chapter. The most common mistake made is simply to get confused between each of the theories, either by remembering the wrong descriptions, the incorrect supporting and criticising studies or by even forgetting which are theories of selective attention and which are theories of divided attention. Before even attempting to revise or write on this topic, you must be sure that you have a good grasp on which theory belongs where. Task 3 will aid your revision in this area.*
- *Don't forget to evaluate your material – only then can you decide which one has the best basis to gain you the higher marks for your essay writing.*
- *Although the main focus here has been on the types of attention, the role of automatic processing and action slips is important and will need to be covered by engaging in wider reading, as recommended below.*

Textbook guide

EYSENCK, M. W. (1993). *Principles of cognitive psychology*. Hove, UK: Psychology Press. Chapter 3 provides extensive coverage on the topic of attention.

EYSENCK, M. W., & KEANE, M. T. (2000). *Cognitive psychology: A student's handbook* (4th ed.). Hove, UK: Psychology Press. Chapter 5 contains more specific research into attention and the evidence on which many of the theories are based.

STYLES, E. A. (1997). *The psychology of attention*. Hove, UK: Psychology Press. Introduces you to a wider range of reading on this topic.

TABLE 2 Theories of Focused Attention				
Name	Theory	Summary	Strengths/ Support	Weaknesses/ Criticisms
Broadbent				
Treisman				
Deutsch & Deutsch				
Johnson & Heinz				
Bottleneck theory				
Kahneman				
Allport				
Baddeley				

2.5

introduction to memory, the multistore model, encoding and retrieval

Core Areas

- Cue dependent forgetting
- Displacement
- Encoding
- Encoding specificity
- Interference
- Long-term memory
- Multistore model
- Recall
- Recognition
- Repression
- Retrieval
- Sensory memory
- Short-term memory
- Storage
- Trace decay
- Two-process theory

Learning Outcomes

By the end of this chapter you should be able to:

- define and understand the key concepts outlined above;
- be able to describe the processes involved in memory including encoding, storage and retrieval and the multistore model (MSM) of memory inclusive of its three memory stores (SM, STM, LTM);
- use the work of the key thinkers in evaluating the MSM;

- understand the different theories of forgetting and the explanations they offer, including their usefulness based on the research evidence provided; and
- distinguish between recall and recognition and acknowledge the key components of the two-process model and encoding specificity.

Running Themes

- Chunking
- Ecological validity
- Experimental cognitive psychology
- Gestalt psychology
- Rehearsal

Introduction

Memory includes three stages:

- ***Encoding****:* occurs during the presentation of material and refers to the way information is coded, for example, if it is visual, auditory or semantic.
- ***Storage****:* how it is stored.
- ***Retrieval****:* how it can be retrieved from memory and whether it is unavailable or simply inaccessible.

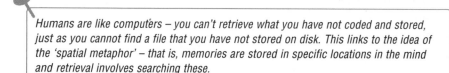

Humans are like computers – you can't retrieve what you have not coded and stored, just as you cannot find a file that you have not stored on disk. This links to the idea of the 'spatial metaphor' – that is, memories are stored in specific locations in the mind and retrieval involves searching these.

The Multistore Model of Memory/Key Thinkers

Atkinson and Shiffrin (1968)

Proposed this model of memory which assumes that there are three separate memory stores (SM, STM and LTM), that information must flow from one store to the next, and that it can only be retained in STM if rehearsal has taken place.

√ Sperling (1960)

Supported the idea that there is a sensory memory store that takes in information from the environment before passing on relevant images to the STM store. He aimed to identify the capacity and duration of SM by showing participants 3 rows of 4 letters for 50 milliseconds using a tachistoscope; in the second condition this occurred alongside a pitched tone corresponding to a particular row of letters. He concluded that the capacity of visual memory is approximately 4 and duration about 200–400 milliseconds, whilst the iconic store retains about 75% of data for 3 seconds.

√ Peterson & Peterson (1959)

Identified that information does only stay in STM for about 15–30 seconds, as demonstrated by the fact that participants who had been asked to learn sets of nonsense syllables and then count backwards showed increasing less recall as the intervals between learning and recall increased from 3–18 seconds. On average, recall was 80% after 3 seconds but this dropped to just 10% after 18 seconds.

✗ Baddeley (1966)

Supported the MSM assumption that encoding for STM is acoustic, whilst in LTM it is based on semantics. This is because when participants were given four sets of either acoustically or semantically similar, or dissimilar, words, it was found that less acoustically similar words were immediately recalled than dissimilar ones, whilst recall 20 minutes later found less semantically similar rather than dissimilar ones were remembered.

√ Miller (1956)

Reviewed and drew evidence from a series of studies conducted by psychologists into the capacity of STM. These studies examined the recall of various types of information sources – tones where the intensity could be varied, patterns of dots or sometimes nonsense syllables or monosyllabic words. There was some variance in the number of items recalled in each of the experiments, but Miller did find that there was a clear and definitive limit at which the immediate digit span worked. There was evidence that the number of items of information to be recalled was indeed approximately seven (plus or minus two). He also found that in order to recall more than simply seven items of information (as would necessarily be the case in everyday situations) it could be chunked. This means that information is put together into units and according to Miller we build larger and larger chunks, with each one containing more information than before. The evidence strongly suggests that STM has a very limited capacity with seven, plus or minus two digits being the limit of most people's immediate digit span.

Murdoch (1962)

Presented participants with a list of words (approximately one per second) and asked them to recall as many as possible. He found that those at the start and at the end of the list were the ones that were remembered. This was called the *serial position effect*: better recall of items at the start of the list was called the *primacy effect* and better recall of items at the end of the list was called the *recency effect*. The study supports the idea of the MSM by showing that there are separate stores and that rehearsal keeps information in STM. It also supports the idea that information flows from one store to the next. This is because the primacy effect occurs as the items at the start of the list have been rehearsed and passed on to LTM, but with the recency effect items are recalled from STM. Middle items are forgotten, as they had not had time for rehearsal (and entered LTM) and had been in memory too long to be retained in STM.

REMEMBER

The multistore model comprises:

➤ SM that takes in information from the environment before passing on relevant images to the STM store
➤ STM, where about 7 chunks of information of an auditory nature are held, for 15–30 seconds
➤ LTM, which is a memory store that processes information according to its meaning (semantically) and which holds an unlimited amount for a lengthy period of time
➤ a flow of information from one store to the next and rehearsal is needed to maintain information in STM.

Handy Hints for Evaluating the multistore model and the work of key thinkers

• It does provide a useful distinction between different memory stores and shows they differ in duration, capacity, forgetting mechanisms and the effects of brain damage.

- It oversimplifies memory, as short- and long-term stores may not be unitary
- LTM itself may not be a unitary store.
- Logie (1999) believes that access to LTM occurs before information is processed in STM.
- Not all psychologists agree that memory is made up of three such separate stores, for example, it is possible that the entire system is controlled by an executive that governs specific tasks or that the level of processing of information is much more important.
- Although rehearsal may be important, Atkinson and Shiffrin do not examine this concept in enough detail, for example, the types of rehearsal that might be used, or consider the distinctiveness of information in relation to this.

Retrieval: Theories of Forgetting

Retrieval can be difficult due to forgetting and was first studied by Ebbinghaus (1885), who learned nonsense syllables and then recalled them at different intervals. He later relearned the list and proposed relearning takes less time, (relearning savings) as some of the early information can, in fact, be retrieved.

Key Thinkers/Theories

Forgetting can either occur because of problems in STM or in LTM

Displacement

Forgetting occurs in the STM because old items have been displaced (replaced) by new pieces of information and therefore the original items are lost. Waugh and Norman (1965) tested if original information (such as digits) can be recalled immediately after learning but are then later forgotten as they have been replaced/displaced or interfered with by other information. They used a probe digit experiment where lists of 16 single digits were used with the last digit in every list acting as the probe. These lists were recorded on tape and presented at either one or four digits per second. The probe digit was also accompanied by a high frequency tone that helped the participant detect that it was the probe. Their task was to write down the digit that followed the probe and rehearsal was controlled as they were told to think only of this last digit. It was found that if the probe was presented near the end of the 16-digit list, then the following digit was remembered far better than if it had been presented at the start of the list. Results therefore showed that material which is not rehearsed is forgotten, despite presentation rate, and that STM has a limited capacity store where new items very quickly displace old ones so that original information is forgotten, which supports the theory because it shows that the later digits were remembered as they had simply replaced the earlier ones.

Trace decay

A theory of forgetting in STM because it states that over time memory traces simply fade away. This can be supported by the Peterson and Peterson study above because this reflects the fact that as time went on (and rehearsal was prevented) the original nonsense syllables simply started to decay.

Repression

Retrieval is impossible due to the threatening nature of material that can't therefore access conscious awareness. This can be supported by Williams (1994), who found that 38% of people who had suffered abuse had no recollection of it 17 years later; however, evidence does show that people can be misled into believing events that never happened.

Interference

There are two types: proactive interference, where old material prevents new information from being remembered and so forgetting occurs due to the interference between the material, and retroactive interference, where new material prevents old information from being remembered and so forgetting occurs due to the interference between the material.

Cue dependent forgetting

Here, information cannot be accessed so it is available but not accessible and can't be rehearsed.

REMEMBER

Theories of Forgetting

➤ Forgetting can be due to problems with STM, where information either fades (trace decay) or gets replaced (displacement).
➤ Alternatively there may be problems with access from LTM because it has been pushed out of consciousness (repression), there is interference or the correct cues are unavailable.

Handy Hints for Evaluating Theories of Forgetting

- It is hard to distinguish between displacement and some of the other theories of forgetting, for example, trace decay theory could account for the findings arguing that traces of the earlier items had simply faded, whilst interference theory would claim that the later digits interfered with the remembering of the first ones.
- Jenkins & Dallenbach (1924) criticised trace decay and argued that forgetting is not a result of the passage of time, since participants who were asked to learn lists and then recalled them after sleeping still recalled more than those who had been tested more immediately. They therefore argued that it is what happens between coding and retrieval that is important rather than time.
- Interference is uninformative about the exact processes involved in forgetting and studies often lack ecological validity since they are laboratory-based.

Retrieval: Recall and Recognition

There are a number of ways in which information can be retrieved, for example:

- **Recall**, which involves searching memory with few external cues.
- **Recognition**, which involves matching material to external information.

Key Thinkers/Theories

Watkins & Gardiner's two-process theory (1979)

Assumes that recall involves a retrieval process followed by a recognition process based on the matching of the retrieved information, but that recognition only involves the matching of material to external information.

As recall involves two stages and recognition only one, then recognition is better.

Handy Hints for Evaluating the Two-Process Model

- Recall can be better than recognition. Muter (1978) found, for example, that people actually recalled names of famous people better than recognising them when asked to circle some from a list (42% versus 29%).
- It doesn't fully explain processes involved in recognition memory.

Encoding specificity

According to Tulving's encoding specificity principle (1983), the overlap between information at recall/recognition and that in the original memory trace will determine retrieval. Therefore, the information overlap between retrieval cues and memory is critical for recall and recognition. Here, context is important.

This was supported by Thomson & Tulving (1970), who found that recall on a task was indeed best, when the cues provided were the same as those provided at input. Recognition was best, as there is a greater relationship between memory test and trace and a greater degree of information overlap is required for successful recall compared to recognition. Sometimes recall is better if information in the recall cue overlaps more than information in the recognition cue with information in the memory trace.

Handy Hints for Evaluating Encoding Specificity

- It is helpful if contextual information is acknowledged (especially the context at learning and on the test).
- However, it is difficult to operationalise or measure overlap, so you end up with circulatory definitions (for example, overlap is inferred from performance).
- Information at retrieval cannot always be compared to information stored in memory, and this explanation of information overlap is not possible.
- Context may not affect recall in the same way it effects recognition. For example, Baddeley (1982) states that intrinsic context impacts information to be remembered but extrinsic context does not. Recall is affected by both, but intrinsic affects only recognition.

Multiple routes

It is too simple to assume that recall and recognition occur in only one way.

Jones (1982) believed that there are two routes to recall: direct, where cues give direct access to information, and indirect, where a cue leads to recall from associations/inferences made.

Similarly, there are two possible routes to recognition (for example, Gardiner & Java, 1993) which can involve recognition on the basis of familiarity or conscious recollection.

Tasks

1 The MSM of memory is often represented diagrammatically. Using the description of the model provided on p. 58 under 'Atkinson & Shiffrin (1968)',draw your own diagram of it. You can then compare this to those provided in your textbook/s.

2 Now, under the headings 'How research supports the MSM' and 'How it can be criticised' record the appropriate evidence using this chapter and your textbooks for guidance. Note, however, that it is not simply asking you to list the studies and criticisms but is focusing on *how* they actually support and criticise.

3 Complete Table 3 on theories of forgetting by providing evidence for and against them.

"To what extent does research support the multistore model of memory?"

It is important to remember that whilst there is much evidence to support this model of memory it is not the only accepted theory and the question therefore requires you to demonstrate a balanced argument. Initially, it would be wise to give a brief outline of the model itself, focusing on its key features, since this then allows you to make logical links between the subsequent supporting evidence. Simply stating the evidence will not gain you marks – you need to say why each piece of evidence you cite supports or criticises the model. Task 2 above is therefore specifically designed to help you think this through and provide you with an essay plan in advance.

"Discuss theories of forgetting"

Although this may at first appear to be a fairly open question, you need to use your understanding of psychology to interpret it. As with other topics,it requires you to both provide an explanation of the theories of forgetting and an evaluation, since unless we know the scientific credibility of the theory, it is hard to judge which of the theories best explains why we forget, and in which circumstances. In a time-limited examination piece you should also note that it will not be possible to cover every one of the theories and if you try to do so it will simply lead to a superficial discussion – mainly focused on outline, rather than allowing you time to engage in discussion of the research that supports or criticises them. Task 3 will ease you into the discussion for this essay.

Common Pitfalls

- There is a huge volume of material associated with this topic and you need to make sure that you are clear about which theories belong where, since confusion can lead to severe inaccuracy when attempting to answer essay questions.
- Remember, that in order to evaluate these studies on memory you will need to also focus on their research methods and therefore understand the key terms involved, such as 'ecological validity'. This is because the applicability of research into memory, beyond a laboratory- based setting, is questionable.
- It would help your understanding to recognise that forgetting can be due to retrieval failure from either STM or LTM and you need to remember that trace decay and displacement are STM theories and the remaining theories more appropriate to LTM.

Textbook guide

BADDELEY, A. D. (1966). Short term memory for word sequences as a function of acoustic, semantic and formal similarity. *Quarterly Journal of Experimental Psychology*, 18, 362–365. This will aid your understanding of the processes involved in memory as a whole but also help underpin your evaluation of the MSM.

BADDELEY, A. D. (1997). *Human memory: Theory and practice* (rev. ed.). Hove, UK: Psychology Press. This provides extremely broad coverage on this topic as a whole.

PETERSON, L. R., & PETERSON, M. (1959) Short term retention of individual verbal items. *Journal of Experimental Psychology*, 58, 193–198. Again, this will allow you to understand the ways in which memory is investigated and focus on the importance of rehearsal and interference. This will therefore help your understanding of memory processes and the topic of forgetting.

TABLE 3   Theories of Forgetting

	Support for theory	Criticisms of theory
Displacement: forgetting occurs in the STM because old items have been displaced (replaced) by new pieces of information and therefore the original items are lost.		
Trace decay: a theory of forgetting in STM because it states that over time memory traces simply fade away.		
Repression: retrieval is impossible due to the threatening nature of material that can't therefore access conscious awareness.		
Interference: there are two types: proactive interference, where old material prevents new information from being remembered, and retroactive interference, where new material prevents old information from being remembered.		
Cue dependent forgetting: here, information cannot be accessed so it is available but not accessible and can't be rehearsed.		

2.6

working memory model

Core Areas

- Articulatory control system
- Central executive
- Inner scribe
- Phonological loop
- Visual cache
- Visuo-spatial scratch pad
- Working memory model

Learning Outcomes

By the end of this chapter you should be able to:

- define the key terms outlined above;
- understand how the three components of the working memory model (WMM) work;
- show an awareness of the experimental evidence to support this theory; and
- be able to evaluate the model using research evidence.

Running Themes

- Cognitive neuroscience
- Ecological validity
- Experimental cognitive psychology
- Gestalt psychology
- Modularity
- Rehearsal
- Schema

Introduction

The WMM is a model of memory proposed by Baddeley and Hitch (1974) to replace the concept of the STM. It instead proposes separate stores of memory, controlled by a central executive, that are responsible for processing auditory and visual data. The central executive is an attentional system that has a limited capacity and is involved in decision making, together with the two slave systems (the articulatory – phonological loop and the visuo-spatial scratch pad). This model is concerned with both active processing and the brief storage of information.

Key Thinkers

Baddeley & Hitch (1974)

According to Baddeley & Hitch the WMM is made up of the:

- **Central executive**: this is a control system and is the most important because It Is responsible for monitoring and coordinating the 'slave systems'. It is flexible as it can process visual and auditory Information (so is modality free) and has some limited storage limited capacity.
- **Phonological Loop**: has an articulatory control system (verbal rehearsal, time-based, inner voice) and a phonological store (speech-based storage system, inner ear). It holds information for a short period of time – so stores a limited number of sounds for brief seconds (an 'inner ear'). It has two components: the phonological store, which stores sound for a brief period of time, and the articulatory control system, Which allows repetition of stored items/is a verbal rehearsal system.
- **Visuo-spatial scratch pad** ('inner eye'): designed for temporary storage and manipulation of spatial and visual information. It has a limited capacity but limits for visual and spatial systems are different (so you can rehearse a set of digits whilst also making spatial decisions). According to Logie (1995), it can be subdivided into the visual cache, which stores information about visual form and colour, and the inner scribe, which holds spatial and movement information

REMEMBER

The WMM comprises the:

➤ **Central executive**: this is a control system that is, modality free and has a limited capacity.

> ➤ **Phonological loop**: has an articulatory control system (verbal rehearsal, time-based, inner voice) and a phonological store (speech-based storage system, inner ear).
> ➤ **Visuo-spatial scratch pad ('inner eye')**: designed for temporary storage and manipulation of spatial and visual information.

Hitch & Baddeley (1976)

Hitch & Baddeley believed that the WMM could be used to predict whether or not two tasks could be performed simultaneously. Their study showed that memory is just one STM unit with responsibility for processing auditory and visual information via a central processor, and as such it could be predicted that only two different tasks can be done at the same time if two different components of the WMM are used. All participants in the study had to answer questions that relied on them using the central executive (so they answered questions such as, 'Does A follow B?' about a letter pair, BA. When participants had to repeat a sequence such as 'the, the, the' or '1, 2, 3, 4, 5, 6' at the same time, little attention or thought was involved. This task uses the articulatory loop. Therefore, in this case there is support for the WMM because the two tasks used different components and could both be done effectively. However, when asked to answer questions on the letter pair (AB) using the central executive and at the same time learn a random set of digits and repeat them (also requiring attention and concentration and therefore using the central executive), this task could not be done. This provides support for the WMM because it shows that there is a complex system consisting of a central control mechanism, which is assisted by slave systems responsible for separated tasks.

Handy Hints for Using Evidence to Support the Central Executive, Phonological Loop and Visuo-spatial Scratch pad

- Evidence has shown that the randomness of sequences produced on presentation tasks decreases as digit memory load increases. This occurs because more demands are being made on the central executive as the number of digits to be remembered increases.
- Baddeley, Thomson & Buchanan (1975) – participants reproduced short words, better than long words, but when asked to prevent use of the phonological loop

by counting repeatedly from one to eight whilst performing a recall task, this effect disappeared with visual but not auditory presentation. This would suggest that the phonological loop does have a passive store concerned with speech perception and an articulatory process linked to this but with access to the phonological store.

- This study accounts well for the word-length effect that irrelevant speech affects recall as do words that sound similar, but it ignores the role of retrieval, and only focuses on rehearsal which is too simplistic.

Handy Hints for Evaluating the Working Memory Model

Weaknesses

- The central executive may not be unitary but may have two or more component systems.
- The role of the central executive is unclear – if it has a limited capacity, what is it?
- One main weakness of the WMM is that *least* is known about the central executive, which is the most important component of the model given that it has an overall regulatory function; for example, it is assumed that it can carry out an enormous variety of processing activities in different conditions, and this makes it difficult to describe its precise function.
- Is the WMM really modality free?
- There is a question of whether there is actually a *single* store or if there are separate visual and spatial systems
- There is also evidence to suggest that verbal and spatial working memory are to some extent separate.

Strengths

- This model is useful as it deals with active processing and transient storage of information and is involved in all complex cognitive tasks.
- It can explain deficits of STM in brain damaged patients.
- The visuo-spatial scratch pad is useful for geographical orientation and for planning special tasks.
- It is generally accepted that the WMM view of STM as a number of different processing units is better than the MSM view that it is a single unit.
- The idea that any one slave system (for example, the phonological loop) may be involved in the performance of very different tasks is a valuable insight.
- It effectively accounts for our ability to store information briefly whilst at the same time actively processing the material.

Tasks

1 Draw a diagram to represent the WMM.

2 Under each of the three components write a few key points to outline their main features.

3 Take each of the bullet points listed under strengths and weaknesses above and state *why* each one is a strength of the model and *why* each one is a weakness.

“Unlike the MSM view of STM as unitary, STM should be seen as comprising of several components that act together like a computer screen or mental workplace. In view of this, critically consider Baddeley & Hitch's WMM”

To answer this question you first of all need to address the key components or description of the WMM and then focus on support for the idea that STM could be seen as having several components. Essentially, this means summarising Baddeley and Hitch's study as an absolute minimum and more importantly using it to discuss how and why it does support the idea that STM may consist of several components. Since all psychology requires you to present a balanced argument, you also need to discuss the possible problems of this model and therefore how the idea that STM has several components can be criticised. In order to do this, as well as the points made in this chapter you may like to discuss methodological issues and opposing memory models such as the MSM and levels of processing (LOP) theories.

Common Pitfalls

- *Students often find this model of memory a difficult one to understand and you therefore need to spend some time getting to grips with the language presented in this chapter and the key components of the model. Without this understanding, it makes it impossible to comprehend fully how the support and criticisms can be used.*
- *It is not sufficient to see this as an isolated topic in memory, but it is really important that you consider it in conjunction with the other models you learn about in your cognitive psychology module, especially since these will aid your evaluation of the WMM.*
- *Remember, that it is critical that you elaborate on how research evidence supports, or how it criticises, the model and do not just list the important points, as this will tell your lecturers nothing about your understanding of the topic and will simply tell them that you are capable of looking up and rewriting information from your textbooks.*

Textbook guide

BADDELEY, A. D. (1996). Exploring the central executive. *Quarterly Journal of Experimental Psychology*, 49A, 5–28. Provides more insight into this component of the WMM.

BADDELEY, A. D. (1997). *Human memory: Theory and practice* (rev. ed.). Hove, UK: Psychology Press. This provides extremely broad coverage on this topic as a whole.

EYSENCK, M. W. & KEANE, M. T. (2000). *Cognitive psychology: A student's handbook* (4th ed.). Hove, UK: Psychology Press (pp. 156–164). Provides excellent coverage on the model, each of the components and the relevant research evidence.

2.7	
episodic and semantic memory	

Core Areas

- Episodic memory
- Semantic memory

Learning Outcomes

By the end of this chapter you should be able to:

- describe each of the types of memory outlined above; and
- understand the extent to which this is a useful distinction based on the appropriate research evidence.

Running Themes

- Cognitive neuropsychology
- Cognitive neuroscience

- Ecological validity
- Experimental cognitive psychology
- Schema
- Semantics

Introduction

Unlike other memory models this one proposes that there are different systems for holding information about the world. This is a theory of LTM.

Key Thinkers

Tulving (1972)

Distinguished between episodic and semantic memory. Episodic memory involves the storage and retrieval of specific events (including place and time). Semantic memory stores information/meaning about the world including general and abstract facts.

> Episodic is a 'knowing when' memory, semantic is a 'knowing what' memory.

Wheeler, Stuss & Tulving (1997)

Believed that episodic memory involves some sort of 'self-knowing', or a special kind of awareness. They also suggested two differences between episodic and semantic memory. Firstly, that episodic memory involves subjective experience of consciously recalling personal events, which is not the case with semantic memory. Secondly, the prefrontal cortex appears to be more involved in episodic memory.

> Support comes from patients with brain damage, for example, Janowsky et al. (1989) looked at memory of frontal lobe patients and found a correlation with amnesia. This suggested that the frontal cortex is involved in episodic memory since specific events could not be recalled.

Handy Hints for Evaluating Episodic and Semantic Memory

- Memory research has made good progress in distinguishing between these two different types of memory.
- However, other explanations can be offered for amnesia in brain damaged patients including general damage to cognitive processes.
- It is difficult to scientifically test something like 'self awareness', especially as it can be difficult to operationalise.

Tasks

1 Reflect on your day. List examples of where you have used episodic and semantic memory.

2 Find at least one other type of support for this distinction in memory (for example, the results of PET scans).

3 List five criticisms of the work on episodic memory and for each point say why they are a criticism.

"To what extent is it useful for psychologists to distinguish between episodic and semantic memory?"

To begin this discussion you need to at least outline Tulving's distinction and describe what is meant by each memory type. The main focus of this question, however, is asking you to weigh up whether or not this is useful and the aim is for you to base your answer on scientific evidence. To do this you could use the information you have collated in tasks 2 and 3 above. It is critical that you do not simply write out the key points but instead really engage with the material and relate it back to how useful the distinction is. So, if using evidence from brain damaged patients, expand and say this shows that the distinction is useful because ...You then need to balance out your argument by doing the same with each of your criticisms/weaknesses. By doing so you will show yourself be a true psychologist evaluating both sides of the argument, using research evidence, before drawing a final conclusion.

Common Pitfalls

- *Since there are two different types of memory you must be careful not to confuse each one.*
- *If you do not have a scientific background you may have to work hard at learning the biological studies associated with this model but not actually be able to understand and therefore discuss why they support the distinction between these two types of memory. If this is the case, spend some time before writing your essays and revising for examinations working out why this is the case.*
- *Remember not to simply list the criticisms but expand on why they criticise the distinction between episodic and semantic memory.*

Textbook guide

TULVING, E., & DONALDSON, W. (1972). *Organisation of memory.* London: Academic Press. Contains specific coverage on the early debate concerning episodic and semantic memory.

WHEELER, M. A., STUSS, D. T., & TULVING, E. (1997). Toward a theory of episodic memory: The frontal lobes and autonoetic consciousness. *Psychological Bulletin, 121*, 331–354. This will aid your evaluation of the theory, allowing you to fully expand on one of the key thinkers in this area.

2.8

learning and memory

Core Areas

- Implicit learning
- Information criterion
- Sensitivity Criterion

Learning Outcomes

By the end of this chapter you should be able to:

- define each of the key terms outlined above;
- understand the suggested criteria for learning to be judged as unconscious; and
- be able to describe and evaluate the work of the key thinkers in this area.

Running Themes

- Cognitive neuropsychology
- Cognitive neuroscience
- Ecological validity
- Experimental cognitive psychology
- Schema
- Semantics

Introduction

Implicit learning can be defined as 'learning complex information without complete verbalisable knowledge of what is learned' (Seger, 1994 in Eysenck & Keane, 2000, p. 63).

> *Put simply, this is learning without conscious knowledge of it.*

When neuroimaging was first used to investigate the area of memory that is associated with implicit learning, various parts of the brain were found to be involved. The most important of these were the motor cortex/motor areas, but there was also some involvement from the premotor cortex and the dorsolateral prefrontal cortex.

Shanks and St John (1994) believed there were two criteria required for learning to be judged as unconscious:

1. ***Information criterion***: information provided by the participant must be responsible for improved performance.

2 **Sensitivity criterion**: must acknowledge that participants may know more than they are being tested on, so underestimate their knowledge as a result.

The problem with this is that it is hard to use these criteria in practice.

Key Thinkers

Berry & Broadbent (1984)

In order to attain a specified level of output, a sugar production factory was managed using complex tasks and it was found that, as predicted by implicit learning theory, these tasks could be performed well, even though the factors leading to performance could not actually be identified or reported by the participants.

Handy Hints for Evaluating Berry & Broadbent's Work

It is, however, possible that people have more conscious awareness and knowledge of these processes than was identified in this study, but simply did not know how to express it.

Tasks

1 Define implicit learning in your own words to check your understanding.

2 Divide a piece of A4 paper in two. On one side give it the heading 'support for implicit learning' and on the other 'criticisms of implicit learning'. Now fill this in with bullet pointed information. You will need to use your textbooks, in addition to this chapter, in order to complete this assignment.

❝Discuss the view that memory is linked to implicit learning❞

First of all you need to show the examiners that you understand the meaning of implicit learning and should therefore define what it is and the criteria that can be used to judge it. Since the question does not, however, just say 'what is implicit learning?' but asks you to discuss how it links to memory, you therefore need to address this directly. Using the evidence above and that researched for task 2, you should then be able to use supporting psychological evidence for the link. Remember, that you also need to balance out your argument by addressing the problems of the supporting evidence, for example, the applicability of laboratory studies within a wider context and the research methods used, as well as the ethics of neurological techniques (see opening chapter).

Common Pitfalls

- *Be aware that implicit learning links to the memory topic and it is not therefore sufficient to discuss it in isolation.*
- *If you are unsure about the biological process and benefits of neurological techniques reread the introductory chapter of this book/your textbook because it is critical to your understanding of the supporting evidence. If you simply rewrite the supporting evidence without fully understanding this, then it will make it hard to truly discuss the links with memory as a whole.*

Textbook guide

GRAFTON, S. HAZELTINE, E., & IVRY, R. (1995). Functional mapping of sequence learning in normal humans. *Journal of Cognitive Neuroscience, 7,* 497–510. A more detailed discussion on the different areas involved in implicit (and explicit) learning.

HOWARD, D. V., & HOWARD, J. H. (1992). Adult age differences in the rate of learning serial patterns: Evidence from direct and indirect tests. *Psychology & Aging, 7,* 232–241. This article will provide specific support for implicit learning.

2.9

speech perception and reading

Core Areas

- Auditory analysis system
- Auditory input lexicon
- Connectionist approach
- Deep dyslexia
- Dual route model
- E-Z reader
- Graphemes
- Neurological evidence
- Phoneme response buffer
- Phonemes
- Phonological dyslexia
- Phonological theory
- Reading
- Recording eye movements
- Semantics
- Semantic system
- Speech output lexicon
- Speech perception
- Surface dyslexia
- Word identification technique

Learning Outcomes

By the end of this chapter you should be able to:

- define and understand the concepts outlined above;
- outline the various techniques used to study reading;

- describe the key models used to explain speech perception and reading and therefore the contributions of the key thinkers; and
- critically consider the usefulness of such explanations.

Running Themes

- Chunking
- Cognitive neuropsychology
- Cognitive neuroscience
- Ecological validity
- Experimental cognitive psychology
- Innate
- Rehearsal
- Schema
- Semantics

Introduction

> *Speech perception and reading differ in a number of ways; there is less reliance on memory in reading and it lacks any clues about meaning etc. that are otherwise provided by prosodic cues in speech (that is, non-verbal information conveyed via pitch, intonation and so on). Reading provides clues only in terms of punctuation, which are less helpful in most cases.*

Techniques used to study the processes involved in reading include:

- **Recording eye movements:** used most commonly, this means measurable data is provided whilst causing minimal intrusion to the participant.
- **Recording reading aloud**: assesses errors more readily than normal reading but results are confounded by the fact that many people feel naturally uncomfortable when doing so; therefore errors are commonly displayed due to this rather than reading abilities per se. It also lacks ecological validity, as reading aloud is a slower process, with more reliance on memory

than silent reading; therefore generalising results from one to the other is unrealistic.

- *Word identification technique*: involves deciding whether letters make up a word (hence word identification) and then saying it aloud.

When reading, our eyes perform rapid jerks or saccades where they move in one direction lasting 10–20 milliseconds, separated by periods of fixation lasting 200–250 milliseconds and spanning approximately 8 letters. Our field of vision (or perceptual span) is affected by the difficulty of the text and print size. Rayner & Sereno (1994) argue that three different spans may be used: total perceptual span, from which information is extracted, letter identification span and word identification span.

REMEMBER

Techniques for studying reading include:

➢ recording eye movements
➢ recording reading errors when reading aloud
➢ identifying words from a sequence of letters.

Key thinkers

Ellis & Young's neuropsychological explanation (1988)

Five different systems are involved in speech production and it can be achieved using three different routes. Basically, sounds/phonemes are extracted using the auditory analysis system, and a mental dictionary is used to recognise familiar words (auditory input lexicon) which are then matched to their meaning (semantic system). Speech is produced via the speech output lexicon and the phoneme response buffer which distinguishes between various speech sounds. Ellis & Young believed that the first route to speaking is the one most commonly used and involves the auditory input lexicon, semantic system and speech output lexicon. Route two can be seen in people with word-meaning deafness, where they can repeat familiar words without understanding their meaning and cannot address non-words because only the auditory analysis system, input lexicon speech output lexicon are used. Alternatively, the third route simply involves converting acoustic (sound) to a phonemic response, and as indicated in people with auditory phonological agnosia a perception and understanding of familiar words is retained, but this is not the case with unfamiliar or non-words.

Reichle, Pollatsek, Fisher & Rayner's E–Z reader model (1998)

Readers assess the familiarity of a word whilst looking at it and this triggers eye movement and lexical access/decisions about the meaning of a word, after which, attention progresses to the following word. Unsurprisingly, lexical and frequency decisions are faster for more common and predictable words. In other words, reading occurs on a word-by-word basis.

Ellis & Young's dual-route model (1988)

The visual system has to initially identify and group sets of letters presented textually, and the process of converting text to sound then involves three routes. Firstly, the grapheme–phoneme conversion occurs where the written word form is converted to sound using punctuation and applying typical rules to translate (groups of) letters. Thus pronunciation of regular spelling-sound words and non-words is possible. Route two involves the lexicon and semantic systems (dictionary and meaning systems). Here, a word is perceived and then a search for its representation is made in the visual input lexicon, following which, its meaning is identified from the semantic system and the word is spoken. Support for the function of this route can be obtained from phonological and deep dyslexics. Lastly, a lexicon-only route can be employed resembling the processes identified above but meaning is not considered; therefore visual input and speech output lexicons are used to produce familiar and regular (rule-based) words (but not unfamiliar and non-words).

Plaut, McClelland, Seidenberg & Patterson's connectionist approach (1996)

Proposed that the pronunciation of all words relies on interactive, rather than separate, mechanisms. Specifically connections exist between visual form and combinations of letters and their basic sound (phonemes). As would then be predicted by this model research showed that naming was more difficult/took longer for inconsistent and rare words, whilst there were few difficulties in pronouncing consistent words because the match was greater between the visual forms and phonemes. Research into surface and phonological dyslexia has provided further support for this model.

> This is a connectionist approach because of the interaction, or connection, between the visual forms and phonemes of words.

Frost's phonological theory of reading (1988)

Emphasised the role of phonological coding (sound) and believed it to be an automatic and fundamental part of reading or processing text, occurring rapidly when a word is presented visually. As such, he predicted that it occurs even if it does not help (or in fact actually impairs) reading.

> Although technically there are three routes in this model, the last two involve sufficiently similar processes hence it is named the dual route instead.

Handy Hints for Evaluating the Work of Key Thinkers

- The E–Z model ignores the role of higher-level cognitive processes involved in reading.
- The dual-route model has many strengths and provides a sensible account of reading that is supported by evidence from dyslexics, thus showing it to have ecological validity. Furthermore, Coltheart, Curtis, Atkins & Haller (1993) modelled it using a computer program and found it was correct 90% of the time compared to 91.5% in humans when assessed using the principles of the dual-route model, and this again lends support to the usefulness of this theory. However, the independent nature of the routes may be criticised and they may not be as distinct as was predicted.
- The phonological theory can be usefully applied to reading processes and appears correct in its assumption that it occurs rapidly and frequently, unlike that proposed by the dual-route model.
- The connectionist approach places a useful emphasis on the idea that reading is more a result of consistency than regularity. However, it does not fully address the role of semantic processing and has experimental limitations, since testing has not focused on words with more than one syllable and would clearly need to be extended before the findings can be generalised more widely.

Tasks

1 Worksheet 2 contains descriptions of each of the main theoretical explanations for speech perception/reading. Fill in the missing

words using those provided at the bottom of the sheet. Some words may be used more than once.

2 Reread Ellis & Young's descriptions of the neuropsychology behind spoken words and the processes involved in reading. Draw an A4 diagram representing the stages involved for each one.

3 Throughout this chapter various types of dyslexia have been mentioned as providing support for the various models of reading. For example, deep, phonological and surface dyslexia. Use your textbooks and library research to outline each type. This chapter tells you which models try to explain the problems encountered by people experiencing these difficulties. Under your definition of each type use this information and your knowledge of the theories to explain why such problems occur. Your course texts for this module will also guide you in this area.

"Discuss psychological explanations of speech perception and/or reading"

Since this essay takes quite a broad spectrum, you will first need to decide which approaches you intend to focus on and give at least some introductory information on the study of these processes, for example, the techniques used to study reading and the differences between this and speech perception. This should literally constitute no more than an opening paragraph, however. The main focus of the title is discussion; it is not therefore asking you to simply rewrite all of your notes on this topic and list everything you know about each theory. Instead, it wants you to discuss the models alongside their supporting evidence and to then balance the argument out by highlighting any possible notes of caution that can be applied to each one. It will also help to consider whether the techniques used resemble reading within the real-life context. In this latter section it will be critical to explain why each point you make supports or criticises the theory it relates to.

"What does research into dyslexia tell us about normal reading processes?"

Since the focal point here is dyslexia, you will need to rely heavily on your completion of task 3 above. Therefore, an introductory paragraph could outline the types of dyslexia. You will then need to use specific research/case studies of people with dyslexia to explain the problems they face with reading, and subsequently use these to highlight the models that can be used to account for normal reading processes. For example, research into surface and phonological dyslexia has provided support for connectionist networks, whilst research into the function of route two of the dual-route model can be obtained from phonological and deep dyslexics. You will need to directly link any case study back to the theory proposed and make links explicit. Such an argument can then be balanced out by the fact that work from single case studies cannot necessarily be generalised to the reading processes of the remainder of the population, and there are some aspects of each of these models that can be criticised. You will therefore need to go on to discuss these before drawing any overall conclusions.

Common Pitfalls

- *The technical terms used in this chapter sometimes pose difficulties for students, which then mean that the theories themselves become very hard to grasp. It is tempting to progress with the chapter because of time constraints but it will certainly hinder essay writing if you do not understand the terms used. This will be quite apparent to the examiner, who will see a lack of elaboration on textbook material, and it will make it especially difficult for you to go on to evaluate material. It is therefore easier and quicker, in the long run, to simply ensure an understanding of the terms in the beginning.*
- *Once the key terms are established, you must then ensure that you do not mix up the various theories of speech perception and reading.*
- *When discussing each theory, you must ensure that you do not slip into purely giving descriptive detail but that you evaluate them using research.*

Textbook guide

ELLIS, A. W., & YOUNG, A. W. (1988). *Human cognitive neuropsychology.* Hove, UK: Psychology Press. Provides much more comprehensive coverage of this whole area and specifically the authors' explanations of reading and speech perception.

HARLEY, T. A. (1995). *The psychology of language: From data to theory.* Hove, UK: Psychology Press. Chapters 2–4 provide a detailed text on the processes involved in speech production and reading and will provide you with much more background information on this topic area.

MILLER-SHAUL, S. (1995). The characteristics of young and adult dyslexic readers on reading and reading related cognitive tasks as compared to normal readers. *Dyslexia, 11 (2),* 132–151. www.pubmed.gov

WORKSHEET 2: EXPLANATIONS OF SPEECH PERCEPTION/ READING

Ellis & Young (1988) – a neuropsychological explanation

Five different systems are involved in speech production and it can be achieved using three different routes. Phonemes are extracted using the _____ and a mental dictionary is used to recognise familiar words _____ which are then matched to their meaning (semantic system). Speech is produced via the _____ and the _____ which distinguishes between various speech sounds. Ellis & Young believed that the first route to speaking is the one most commonly used and involves the_____. Route two can be seen in people with word-meaning deafness, where they can repeat familiar words without understanding their meaning and cannot address non-words because only the _____ are used. Alternatively, the third route simply involves converting_____

Reichle et al. (1998) – E–Z reader model

Readers assess the familiarity of a word whilst looking at it and this triggers _____ about the meaning of a word, after which, attention progresses to the following word.

Ellis & Young (1988) – dual-route model

The visual system has to initially identify and group sets of letters presented textually and the process of converting text to sound then involves three routes. Firstly, the _____ occurs where the written word is converted to sound using punctuation and applying typical rules to translate (groups of) letters. Thus pronunciation of regular spelling-sound words and non-words is possible. Route two involves the _____. Here, a word is perceived and then a search for its representation is sought in the visual input lexicon, following which, its meaning is identified from the semantic system and the word is spoken. Lastly, a lexicon-only route can be employed resembling the processes identified above but meaning is not considered, therefore visual input and speech output lexicons are used to produce familiar and regular (rule-based) words (but not unfamiliar and non-words).

Plaut et al. (1996) – connectionist approach

Connections exist between _____ and combinations of letters and their _____.

Frost (1998) – phonological theory of reading

Emphasised the role of _____ and believed it to be an automatic and fundamental part of reading or processing text, occurring rapidly when a word is presented visually. As such, he predicted that it occurs even if it does not help (or in fact actually impairs) reading.

Visual form

acoustic (sound) to a phonemic response

speech output lexicon

phoneme response buffer

lexicon and semantic systems (dictionary and meaning systems)

auditory input lexicon

eye movement and lexical access/decisions

Phonological coding

auditory analysis system,

auditory analysis system, input lexicon speech output lexicon

grapheme–phoneme conversion

Phonemes

auditory input lexicon, semantic system and speech output lexicon

2.10

language comprehension

Core Areas

- Bridging inferences
- Capacity theory
- Coherence assumption
- Constraint-based theory
- Discourse processing
- Effort-after-meaning
- Elaborated propositional net
- Elaborative inferences
- Event indexing model
- Explanation assumption
- Garden path model
- Illocutionary force
- Locutionary force
- Minimalist hypothesis
- Parsing
- Perlocutionary force
- Pragmatics
- Proposition
- Propositional net
- Propositional representation
- Reader goal assumption
- Reconstructive memory
- Schema
- Script-pointer-plus-tag hypothesis
- Search-after-meaning theory
- Semantic representation
- Sentence processing
- Situational representation
- Surface representation

Learning Outcomes

By the end of this chapter you should be able to:

- define the key terms outlined above;
- understand that language comprehension can be viewed by looking at sentence processing (garden path, constraint-based and capacity theories), discourse processing (search-after-meaning and minimalist hypothesis) and story processing (schema and script-pointer-plus-tag explanations, discourse processing, construction integration and event indexing theories); and
- show an awareness of the strengths and weaknesses offered in terms of explaining language comprehension.

Running Themes

- Bottom-up processing
- Ecological validity
- Experimental cognitive psychology
- Gestalt psychology
- Schema
- Semantics
- Top-down processing

Introduction

Sentence processing

Sentence processing involves:

1 **Analysis of syntax – or grammatical structure ('set of rules')**: this is known as ***parsing***. Grammatical structure can be ambiguous in terms of comprehension either at a *global* level (the sentence has more than one interpretation) or at the *local* level (varying interpretations could be made at different stages of processing).

2 **Analysis of semantics – or meaning (pragmatics)**: pragmatics refer to how language is used to communicate a message and it

is argued that a sentence has three different types of force/meaning: locutionary force (literal meaning) and illocutionary force (goal/intended meaning) and perlocutionary force (actual effect). So, to comprehend language all of these must be used.

Processing sentences involves looking at the 'set of rules' it uses and its meaning.

Key Thinkers

Frazier & Rayner's garden path model (1982)

One element of a sentence is considered (the simplest one) because this involves minimal attachment (for example, has the fewest sentence parts) and then late closure occurs (where new words are attached to the phrase). Therefore, meaning or prior content does not affect selection.

MacDonald, Perlmutter & Seidenberg's constraint-based theory (1994)

Parallel processes operate and are constrained by semantic and grammatical knowledge, and analyses of these is therefore simultaneous. When a sentence is ambiguous, four assumptions are made/used: grammatical knowledge of possible intent, association of words are not independent, ambiguity, and past experience determines interpretations made.

Just & Carpenter's capacity theory (1992)

Focuses on working memory (or the central executive that deals with language comprehension in the WMM). Working memory stores and processes language in a limited capacity during processing; therefore the main assumption is that when people are assessed using reading span tasks there are individual differences in their language comprehension because there are individual differences in their working memory capacity. MRI work also shows that the same areas of the brain are involved in reading span as in sentence comprehension and that there is more activity in Wernicke's area when asked to read and maintain information rather than reading it alone.

REMEMBER

Comprehension of Sentences

➤   The simplest part of a sentence is considered and then new words are attached to the phrase.
➤   Parallel processes operate and are constrained by semantic and grammatical knowledge, and analyses of these is therefore simultaneous.
➤   Working memory stores and processes language in a limited capacity; therefore there are individual differences in language comprehension because there are individual differences in people's working memory capacity.

Handy Hints for Evaluating Theories of Sentence Processing

- The garden path model provides a simple account of how sentences are processed but it may be incorrect to assume that semantics play no role in this process; it also ignores factors such as punctuation, rhythm and so on. Focusing purely on minimal attention and late selection is too narrow.
- Constraint-based theories are useful because it is apparent that different grammatical interpretations are made by different people when given a sentence and the theory therefore shows ecological validity; however, it is too unspecific about the detail of syntactic processing. Also, there is little empirical evidence for parallel representations and it is difficult to test empirically.
- Just & Carpenter (1992) were able to support their capacity theory using experimental evidence. They measured the reading time of various sentences and found that people with low reading span made little use of meaning but people with high reading span did, thus supporting the idea that the latter had a greater working memory capacity able to attend to sentence meaning. However, it is also possible that those with large capacities also try and interpret all sentence ambiguities until disproved, therefore making comprehension harder than making a single interpretation.
- The capacity theory can, however, be criticised because the relationship between reading span and language comprehension is only correlational, which poses problems as cause and effect cannot be assumed. In other words, you cannot prove the relationship – some argue that language processing ability and comprehension determines working memory capacity rather than vice versa. We don't know if differences are innate or due to experience, and the theory does not really account for the processes involved in language comprehension but more on the capacity in working memory.

You will notice that these hints show both the strengths and weaknesses of each of the explanations.

Discourse Processing

Discourse is written text or speech that is the more common form of language comprehension required in real life. So it has higher ecological validity than looking at such comprehension purely in relation to sentences. The role of inferences ('the core of the understanding process' – Schank, 1976 in Eysenck & Keane, 2000, p. 168) is important in such research, especially bridging inferences, which link current and preceding text, and elaborative inferences, which enhance understanding with detail.

Language comprehension necessarily requires active cognitive processing and involvement.

Key Thinkers

Graesser, Singer & Trabasso's search-after-meaning theory (1994)

Readers use their goals to give meaning to text and then use these to explain and comprehend actions/events in the text. Specifically, it involves giving meaning to the text based on goals (reader goal assumption); this has to be coherent (coherence assumption) and is used to explain events (explanation assumption).

McKoon & Ratcliff's minimalist hypothesis (1992)

States that inferences are automatic (where general knowledge is used to combine sentences coherently, or where information is explicit in the text or where they are directed and are therefore formed to achieve a goal). This is different to constructionist hypotheses, as it is predicted that there are constraints on the number of automatic inferences that are made.

Story Processing

In order to comprehend a story, evidence has shown that we interpret some aspects and leave out others – mainly focusing on important events.

> Within this is a 'story grammar' – or a set of rules from which the structure of the story is derived, usually in a hierarchy of importance, for example, plot before characters.

Key Thinkers

Bartlett's schemas and reconstructive memory (1932)

Bartlett believed that schemas (the building blocks of knowledge derived from previous experience) were fundamental for language comprehension. Based on his storytelling of an Indian folk tale, 'War of the Ghosts', he found that we do not in fact recall information accurately but instead reconstruct language based on such expectations ('effort after meaning'). Accounts of the story were distorted in several ways by westerners, for example, omissions were made, there were changes of order, rationalisation, alterations in importance and distortions of emotion.

Schank & Abelson's script-pointer-plus-tag hypothesis (1977)

Developed Bartlett's ideas in that they still focused on schemas and scripts, but Eysenck and Keane (2000) state that they redeveloped some of the ideas to suggest that there is a combining of material from the story and schema and note is made of typical or untypical actions within the story (that is, whether or not they are consistent with these underlying scripts). Recognition memory and recall is then better for atypical actions because they are easier to discriminate and thus are tagged individually in memory. However, over time typical actions are better recalled because of their link to well-established schemas.

Kintsch & Van Dijk's discourse processing (1978)

To comprehend language, analyses are made both of the argument (semantic representation) and of the position (giving meaning to the smallest component of a story, for example, a phrase within it). These meanings are given as a result of processing within a limited capacity STM store and bridging inferences amongst other things. Therefore, important propositions most relevant to understanding the story have subsequently

better recall because they spend longer in this buffer. Irrelevant propositions are deleted, generalised or single propositions constructed from
numerous ones. Discourse occurs at two processing levels: micro (where
the smallest components are connected) and macro (where the story is
formed by editing the smaller details to give an overall picture.

Kintsch's construction integration model (1988, 1992, 1994)

Propositions derive from sentences and enter a short-term buffer
(propositional net). Inferences are then added from LTM leading to an
elaborated propositional net (inclusive of irrelevant details). An integration process then occurs where connected structures are selected to form
text representations stored in episodic text memory. So, if two pieces of
information were processed together in the original short-term buffer
store, then the relationship between them will have been retained
throughout the process. Therefore, discourse processing/language comprehension uses three levels of representation: surface representation
(actual text), propositional representation (text-based propositions) and
situational representations (a mind map/mental model based on
schemas constructed from the situational representations in the text).

Zwaan & Radvansky's event indexing model (1990)

To understand stories/comprehend language several aspects are analysed:
the protagonist, the relationship between current and past events, the relationship between such events and their spatial relationship and the relationship between goals and previous events. In other words, temporality,
causality, spatiality and intentionality. It is difficult to comprehend or construct an idea of the situation if these aspects do not match up.

Handy Hints for Evaluating Explanations of Story Processing

- Bartlett's work lacks empirical testability, as it did not follow a particularly
  rigorous scientific procedure and it is therefore difficult to precisely measure,
  replicate or generalise the findings. The study also lacks ecological validity, as
  in real life language comprehension and recall usually has some meaning for us.
- The script-pointer-plus-tag hypothesis provides a useful extension to Bartlett's
  work, but it is difficult to truly operationalise schemas and therefore this
  theory again lacks empirical testability.
- The discourse processing model doesn't say how propositions or bridging inferences are formed in the beginning and there is no acknowledgement of the fact
  that the process must necessarily involve more than just linking propositions.

- The construction integration model extends language comprehension beyond propositional representation and looks at the role of schemas/mental models concerned with the situation. It therefore looks more coherently at the linking of prior and current knowledge compared to other theories. However, the limited processing capacity may sometimes actually prevent situational representations from being formed. It is also difficult to test the idea that some information is included in the early stages and other information disregarded.
- The event indexing model ignores the interaction between the events and is too reductionist to separate them.

REMEMBER

Theories of Story Processing

➢ We reconstruct language based on expectations ('effort after meaning'); this causes omissions to be made, changes of order, rationalisation, alterations in importance and distortions of emotion.

➢ Recognition memory and recall is then better for atypical actions because they are easier to discriminate and thus are tagged individually in memory.

➢ Analyses are made both of the argument (semantic representation) and of the position (giving meaning to the smallest component of a story).

➢ Propositions derive from sentences and enter a short-term buffer (propositional net) and inferences are then added from LTM leading to an elaborated propositional net (inclusive of irrelevant details). An integration process then occurs where connected structures are selected to form text representations stored in episodic text memory.

➢ Several aspects are analysed including the protagonist, temporality, causality, spatiality and intentionality.

Tasks

1 Read Eysenck & Keane (2000, p. 348) Produce an A4 piece on how McKoon & Ratcliff (1986) support the minimalist hypothesis and why criticisms can be made of the constructionist position.

2 Complete Table 4 by summarising the approaches to language comprehension.

3 Using the list provided at the start of this chapter, produce a list of definitions/key terms that you have encountered in this chapter.

"Language comprehension involves many different elements. Discuss psychological theories that have attempted to understand this process."

Since this is a rather large topic area, the first and most important task is to decide which aspect/s of language comprehension you wish to deal with in your essay. A general introduction should indicate that you understand the topic to have greater depth than your forthcoming coverage and then you need to outline the areas you will focus on. The question asks you to discuss the relevant theories, 'discuss' meaning both describe and evaluate each one. You therefore first need to show the examiners that you understand what each theory actually proposes and you may wish to give actual examples. Secondly, you need to take a critical approach to each one and elaborate on the strengths and weaknesses. Task 2 above should help you in this, but when transferring this information to an essay, it is critical that you expand upon it and show the examiners that you understand how the points you make relate to the overall discussion on language comprehension.

Common Pitfalls

- *This is a complex topic that requires you to have a good comprehension of the technical terms before writing about them.*
- *Different aspects of language comprehension are tackled in this chapter and you need to make sure that you are aware of the differences in comprehending sentences versus stories; too often students simply lump all material together such that there is little coherent structure in writing or, indeed, in revision.*
- *In any large topic the temptation is to start writing out every possible theory that you remember and actually forget that it is equally important to consider what is good or bad about any theory; therefore when discussing them, it is essential that you use your analytical skills and weigh up their strengths and weaknesses.*

Textbook guide

CSI.PSYCHOL.CAM.AC.UK/INDEX.HTML An up-to-date website of the research into language being conducted by the Centre for Speech and Language at Cambridge University.

HARLEY, T. (2001). *The psychology of language* (2nd ed.). Hove, UK: Psychology Press.

JUST, M. A., & CARPENTER, P. A. (1992). A capacity theory of comprehension. *Psychological Review, 99* 122–149. Looks at the originally proposed capacity theory in more detail and gives specific procedural detail of the supporting experimental work.

TABLE 4 Approaches to Language Comprehension

Approach	Description	Strengths	Weaknesses
Garden path theory			
Constraint-based			
Capacity theory			
Search-after-meaning			
Minimalist			
Schema			
Script-pointer-plus-tag			
Discourse processing			
Construction integration			
Event indexing			

| 2.11 | |
| language (speech) production | |

Core Areas

- Agrammatism
- Anomia
- Anticipatory errors
- Aphasia
- Broca's area
- Co-operative principle
- Exchange errors
- Lexicon
- Lexicon bias
- Morphological encoding
- Perseverated errors
- Phonetic encoding
- Phonological encoding
- Prosodic cues
- Semantics
- Spreading activation theory
- Syntactics
- WEAVER++ (Word-form Encoding by Activation and VERification)
- Wernicke's area

Learning Outcomes

By the end of this chapter you should be able to:

- define the key terms;
- understand what speech errors tell us about normal language production;
- outline and evaluate the models of language production offered by the key thinkers in this area, including the spreading activation model, anticipation

and perseverated errors and WEAVER++ (Word-form Encoding by Activation and VERification); and

- critically discuss the neurological evidence into this area, including the parts of the brain involved in speech production, and Broca's area and Wernicke's area.

Running Themes

- Bottom-up processing
- Cognitive neuropsychology
- Cognitive neuroscience
- Ecological validity
- Experimental cognitive psychology
- Schema
- Semantics
- Top-down processing

Introduction

Language is produced with an aim in mind, so language production is goal-directed. Most importantly, the co-operative principle (Grice, 1967) predicts that speakers and listeners must co-operate when producing language and ideally, cues such as rhythm, stress and intonation (prosodic cues) are used.

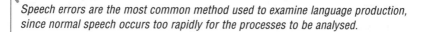

Speech errors are the most common method used to examine language production, since normal speech occurs too rapidly for the processes to be analysed.

Most theories assume that speech is pre-planned, using a series of processing stages from a general intention to produce a sound through to its actual production.

Key Thinkers

Spreading activation theory, Dell (1986), Dell & O'Seaghdha (1991)

The theory predicts that several common errors will be made in speech production. Principally, they are anticipatory errors (where words are spoken 'in anticipation' too early in the sentence and exchange errors (where words are 'exchanged' or swapped around), although multiple errors are possible. The lexical bias effect suggests that errors in language production are made using either actual words or basic word forms. This is because speech production involves more advanced processing at the highest of the four levels of processing, that is, at the semantic/meaning level not at the syntactic/grammatical level, morphological/basic word forms and phonological level, and errors occur because incorrect items are sometimes activated more readily than correct ones.

Dell, Schwartz, Martin, Saffran & Gragnon's anticipation and perseverated errors (1997)

Developed the above theory and specifically outlined anticipatory and perseverated errors as those most common in language production (words being spoken either before or after they should have been). As such, anticipatory errors are most common in experts who are planning delivery of speech and perseverated errors and less common because of prior experience/practise.

WEAVER++ (Word-form Encoding by Activation and VERification), Levelt (1989), Levelt, Roelofs & Meyer (1999)

Speech production occurs because there is an activation-spreading network that involves lexical concepts and nodes for abstract words (lemmas), derived from a mental dictionary, and where there are nodes containing general units of meaning (morphemes) and sounds (phonemics). According to this model, speech is produced once the following series of processes have taken place: firstly, conceptual preparation and lexical selection; secondly, morphological, phonological, phonetic and phonemic encoding; and, finally, encoding. In other words, general meaning leads to the processing of abstract words which then help to select basic word forms, following which, syllables are compiled, speech sounds prepared and then the actual word is produced. Initially, therefore, the mental dictionary allows a decision about word production and then specific details concerning syllables and pronunciation follow.

REMEMBER

Theories of Speech Production

➢ Speech production involves four levels of processing and the spreading activation of material at the highest of these levels (semantic); errors therefore occur because incorrect items are sometimes activated more readily than correct ones.

➢ Anticipatory and perseverated errors occur most commonly in language production (words being spoken either before or after they should have been).

➢ General meaning leads to the processing of abstract words which then help to select basic word forms, following which, syllables are compiled, speech sounds prepared and then the actual word is produced.

Handy Hints for Evaluating the Work of Key Thinkers

- Spreading activation theory has many strengths, especially as its basis has been successfully tested experimentally. Processes such as word recognition can be linked to this theory and thus a broadened emphasis can be made to cognitive processes as a whole, showing that it is clearly rooted within cognitive psychology. However, instead of focusing at the outset on language production as a whole, it looks somewhat narrowly at speech errors (rather than normal speech production) and does so by looking at specific word errors instead of the wider construction of general language. Widely applying this, therefore, poses difficulties.
- As can be seen in the section below, evidence for anticipation and perseveration errors can be found in patients with speech problems and this lends support to the idea that the theory has some substantial basis.
- Like the theories mentioned above, WEAVER++ has been well supported by research, especially regarding the speed and serial nature of processing, and unlike those above, it attempted more readily to address normal speech production rather than simply focusing on errors. Again, however, it looks more at single words instead of sentences and more critically, one must be cautious about applying a computer-based theory to human speech processes.

Neuropsychological/Neuroscientific Research and Speech Production

Research has examined the language production of people suffering from many language disorders. For example: when people are unable to name objects (anomia); where grammatical structure is lacking in production, even though people have a knowledge of appropriate words (agrammatism), or where the opposite is true and grammar is in place but the right words are lacking, whereby people may even resort to using made up words; and lastly aphasia, where language is understood but cannot be produced (jargon aphasia) or there are difficulties in understanding language (fluent aphasia).

Overall, the evidence presented does support the theories of speech production outlined above, for example, errors in naming objects may indeed occur because word selection presents difficulties. PET scans and post-mortem evidence suggest that specific areas of the left hemisphere are responsible for language production in 'normal' individuals (Wernicke's area being of particular importance in recognising and interpreting meaning and Broca's area is implied in the formation of spoken words) and thus left hemispheric damage was originally believed to account for deficits in speech production.

Eysenck and Keane (2000, p. 375) neatly summarise the conclusions as follows: 'findings from anomic patients have indicated the value of two-stage theories of lexicalisation. Agrammatical aphasics and jargon aphasics provide evidence for separate stages of syntactic planning and content-word retrieval in speech production.'

> *This evidence does not, however, mean that a person with problems in speech production will have difficulties with comprehension, and individual differences need to be considered, since there are wide variations within, as well as between, patients suffering from such disorders. Localisation of brain functioning is not always clear-cut and there are many limitations of the methods used to specify brain activity.*

Tasks

1 Read the sections outlining the key features of the spreading activation model and Levelt's Weaver++/approach. Draw a diagram representing each model/the processes and stages involved.

2 Use your textbooks to produce an A4 page of supporting evidence for each of the three theories. Then, on the back of each page extend your notes by explicitly writing a paragraph starting:'This evidence provides support for the _____ theory because...'

"Discuss the view that studying speech errors has offered valuable information regarding speech production"

The emphasis in this question is specifically on those theories of production that deal with errors, and thus the spreading activation model is the key to the title. It requires that you initially outline some of the evidence into speech errors (use the evidence you have compiled for task 2 above) and then, more critically, specify what it actually tells us about production. In other words, you need to show that they highlight the fact that speech production involves four levels of processing and the spreading activation of material at the highest of these levels (semantic) and that errors therefore occur because incorrect items are sometimes activated more readily than correct ones. You will also need to go on to address the difficulties associated with this approach, for example, its focus more on individual words than on language production overall. Rather than simply listing the problems, however, note that the question asks you to 'discuss'. You therefore need to expand upon the problems and engage with the material, using them directly in relation to the question and thus saying why it casts doubt on the notion that research provides valuable insight into speech production. Additionally, you could go on to address the neuropsychological evidence in this area and show how research into aggrammatism, anomia and aphasia has highlighted the areas of the brain involved in speech production (for example, Broca's and Wernicke's areas). Again, any such discussion must be balanced out with the idea that although such evidence is valuable in understanding speech production, it may not be as clear-cut as at first appears. Every opportunity should be taken to refer your material back to the question you have been asked to answer.

"Discuss the approaches to speech production"

This question has a very different emphasis to the one above and allows for a wider scope of discussion. Here, all of the main theories can be covered (albeit using the same format as above, and in other topics). The options are to include discussion of both the spreading activation theory, anticipation and perseverated errors and WEAVER++. The question asks you to provide a concise description of each model and then go on to evaluate it by providing supporting evidence and any criticisms of the theory. In order to do this, it is not sufficient to simply rewrite your notes; you are required to engage in the material – expanding on exactly how each point you make supports or criticises the theory you have outlined. It would then be useful to round the essay off by drawing some conclusion about the way in which speech is produced.

Common Pitfalls

- *One of the most common pitfalls in this area is for students who lack a background in biology to ignore the neuroscientific evidence because they find it difficult to understand and therefore focus upon only half the evidence (that is the psychological explanations). It is important, however, that even a basic understanding of this area is obtained.*
- *There are quite a few complex terms in this chapter and they are fundamental to any understanding of the theories. If this is an area that you feel you might struggle with, then it is worth writing out each of the key definitions provided at the start of this chapter.*
- *Do not forget that psychology requires you to be an analyst of all evidence presented to you. You will need to be able to provide research evidence to support each of the theories on language production and also be able to criticise the work, especially the notion of applying work on speech errors and computer programs to the development of normal speech.*

Textbook guide

CARROLL, D. W. (1999). *Psychology of language* (3rd ed.). Pacific Grove, CA: Brooks/Cole. Chapter 8 provides more information and wider reading on the area of speech production and language.

HARLEY, T. (2001). *The psychology of language* (2nd ed.). Hove, UK: Psychology Press. Provides a much more detailed discussion on this topic.

RUGG, M. (1997). *Cognitive neuroscience.* Hove, UK: Psychology Press. Provides an excellent chapter on the contribution of neuroscience to our understanding of language, which has been only briefly discussed in this chapter.

2.12

problem-solving

Core Areas

- Algorithmic methods
- Anti-looping strategy
- Balance strategy
- Functional fixedness
- Gestalt theories
- Heuristic methods
- Information processing approach
- Insight
- Means–ends analysis
- Problem-space theory
- Rule application hypothesis
- Rule learning hypothesis
- Tower of Hanoi

Learning Outcomes

By the end of this chapter you should be able to:

- define the key terms outlined above;
- show an understanding of the processes involved in problem-solving using Gestalt and information processing explanations;
- relate these explanations to the problem-solving tasks set by the key thinkers including the water jug problem, problem space theory, Tower of Hanoi problem and the missionaries and cannibals problem; and
- be able to evaluate each of the different explanations of problem-solving.

Running Themes

- Bottom-up processing
- Ecological validity
- Experimental cognitive psychology
- Schema
- Semantics
- Top-down processing

Introduction

Problem-solving makes use of cognitive processes to achieve a goal.

> *To solve problems, a person's thinking involves a level of consciousness of their thoughts. It may be directive (thinking about a specific goal) or more indirective and may use/have different expectations of knowledge.*

Originally, behaviourists thought that problems were solved through trial and error. Subsequent approaches include the Gestalt approach and the information processing approach.

Gestalt Approach

Eysenck & Flanagan (2001) summarise the approach as follows;

- Problem-solving is both reproductive and productive.
- Reproduction uses previous experience.
- Productive problem-solving involves sudden insight into the structure of the problem and its productive restructuring.

Kohler (1927) found that insight was shown by chimps when they attached two sticks together to reach a banana that was placed outside their cage, thus questioning early explanations offered by learning theorists on problem-solving by trial and error.

Functionalfixedness/mental set is a problem that occurs when problem-solving becomes difficult. It therefore appears that we each develop our own 'problem-solving set'.

Key Thinkers

Maier's 'pendulum problem' (1931)

People were brought into a room where there were two lengths of string hanging from the ceiling and a number of objects lying about, for example, poles, pliers, extension cables. Their task was to tie the strings together; however, the strings were too far apart to reach each other. The pendulum problem can be insightfully solved by tying pliers to the ends of the strings and swinging both to catch them in the middle.

This supports the Gestalt idea of problem-solving, as they had to restructure the problem in a number of ways, for example, recognise it as a problem, accidentally find part of the solution and then establish a fixed answer derived from the reorganisation of thinking made at this stage.

Luchins & Luchins's 'water jug' problem (1959)

There were two groups. One was given problems that could be solved using the same solution repeatedly and the other, problems that required different solutions. A subsequent problem could then be solved either very simply or using the solution already employed by the experimental group. The experiment supported the idea that mental set is fixed, as this group used their established method rather than perceiving the simple solution.

Handy Hints for Evaluating the Gestalt Approach

- This approach is useful, as it shows that problem-solving is more than trial and error.
- But the concepts used to solve problems are non-specific, for example, how does insight result from reorganisation?
- It is inevitable that some reproductive application of problem-solving is helpful in the solution of everyday problems and that the behaviourists were therefore correct in their assumptions and processes of problem-solving without insight.

Key Thinkers – Information Processing Approach

Ohlsson (1992)

LTM is activated in the course of solving a particular problem and information relating to possible solutions or actions is retrieved and interpreted according to how the problem is currently structured. When the problem is represented in a way that does not allow retrieved information to perceive new solutions, then a block occurs and this can only be overcome when the representation is changed. This occurs when new information about the problem is added, when perceptual constraints are removed or material is re-encoded. As such, insight is the result of overcoming this block and retrieving sufficient knowledge to solve the problem.

This ignores individual differences, for example, people with high IQ and with expertise about a problem are capable of changing the way a problem is presented more ably/quickly.

Newell & Simon's problem-space theory (1972)

Problems have a structure that can be viewed as a set of states (initial-goal state). Operations are applied (actions taken) that move one through these problem-solving states, sometimes leading to dead ends, other times to discovery such that movement occurs towards the goal. People use their knowledge and heuristics to do this, so a person's prior knowledge is crucial to their problem-solving.

It is called the problem-space theory because the idea is that there is a whole space full of intermediate states during which problem-solving occurs towards the end goal/solution.

Newell & Simon's Tower of Hanoi (1972)

When shown three vertical pegs in a row, people were asked to reallocate three size-ordered discs from the first to the last peg (initial-goal state). However, there are a number of set rules when solving this problem, only one disc can be moved at a time and a larger disc cannot go on top of a smaller one. In order to solve this, people therefore had to use the mental operations outlined in the above approach. It emerged from this task that people use various methods of problem-solving:

- **Heuristic methods**: 'rules of thumb' that often produce a solution. The *means–ends analysis* is one of the most important heuristic methods and involves recognising the difference between current and goal states, creating a subgoal to reduce this and then selecting an operator to solve the subgoal (Eysenck & Flanagan, 2001).
- **Algorithmic methods**: based on principles that encourage a systematic search through every possible solution. Although this offers a guaranteed solution, the problem lies in the fact that it is very time consuming.

Anzai & Simon (1979)

When solving the Tower of Hanoi they stated that people use specific strategies – domain independent strategies that include a loop avoidance – where a sequence of states and moves towards a goal can be made without backtracking and where they help form more stable sequences which can help solve this problem, and later ones.

Simon & Reed's missionaries and cannibals problem (1976)

They believed three specific heuristics could be used to solve this problem. People were asked how three missionaries and three cannibals can cross a river when the boat holds a maximum of two and where more cannibals than missionaries cannot be left on the bank otherwise the missionaries will be eaten. The heuristics were: *balance strategies* (equal numbers of each remain); *means–ends strategy* (used in an attempt to reach the sub goal); and *anti-looping* strategies (which avoid backtracking on moves already made towards solutions). The most critical move is the transition made from balance to means–ends.

REMEMBER

Problem-solving Approaches

- ➤ Gestalt theorists believe problem-solving is both reproductive and productive, so uses previous experience and sudden insight as well as restructuring of the problem.
- ➤ Problems have a structure that can be viewed as a set of states (initial-goal state). Operations are applied (actions taken) that may alternatively involve moves through the problem-solving states towards the goal.

> ➤ Heuristic methods or 'rules of thumb' often produce a solution, as do algorithmic methods, which encourage a systematic search through every possible solution.

Handy Hints for Evaluating the Information Processing Approach

- Experimental testing lacks ecological validity, as problem-solving in real life often involves less well-defined problems.
- None of the above methods can be guaranteed to solve a problem.
- There are difficulties in applying theories in practice. For example, means–ends analysis was incorporated into the GPS (general problem solving) computer program that imitated problem solving steps supposedly applied by humans, but was discontinued as it was found that it did not in fact transfer.

REMEMBER

Other factors that affect problem solving:

> ➤ **Rule application hypothesis (Hayes & Simon, 1977):** the easier the rules are to apply to the problem, then the more quickly and easily it will be solved.
> ➤ **Rule Learning Hypothesis Kotovsky, Hayes & Simon, (1985):** problems will also be solved more easily when the rules for solving them are clearer and quick to pick up.

Tasks

1 Think of a problem you have recently solved, for example, where to go on holiday in the summer. Brainstorm/discuss the steps involved in solving this problem. Now use the explanations offered in this chapter to see if you can apply them to your own example. Were there any difficulties in doing so?

2 To widen your understanding of problem-solving use your textbook to write up one A4 page on how experts solve problems (for example, chess players).

" Describe two studies investigating problem-solving and discuss the extent to which they contribute to our theoretical understanding of the nature of solving problems. "

This question can be tackled by focusing on two specific sections. They are, however, linked, so it is important to see them as a whole. Therefore, If you take two studies, it is best to do so on the basis of those that will open the broadest discussion in terms of theoretical explanations. It would be useful to select, for example, the water jug problem and the Tower of Hanoi, as this will then allow you to highlight that our theoretical understanding of this area involves two different approaches – the Gestalt approach and the information processing approach. Furthermore, you can expand on this by examining the role of heuristics and algorithmic methods. Since you are asked to discuss the extent to which they contribute to our understanding, you will need continuously to refer your material back to the question and say how it helps, but remember that every argument should be balanced by an evaluation of any possible difficulties in using these approaches. You can use the Handy Hints provided in this chapter to do this, but, most critically, remember that you will only gain the higher marks if you go beyond just listing those hints and instead say why each one poses difficulties.

Common Pitfalls

- *There are many different examples of problem-solving and it is essential that you are clear on what tasks each involves, because this is fundamental to the approach you will then go on to link them to.*
- *If it helps you, draw the tasks diagrammatically so that you picture both the task itself and possible solutions.*
- *Since there is an overlap between some of the key terms in this chapter and the subsequent one on decision making (heuristics, for instance), then you need to understand the relevance specifically to problem-solving.*
- *As with all cognitive topics, do not just take the explanations offered at face value but take a critical approach – show an understanding of the psychological evidence to support each of the explanations and the notes of caution/ecological validity of such work.*

Textbook guide

GILHOONY, K. J., & HOFFMAN, R. (EDS) (1998). *Expert thinking*. Hove, UK: Psychology Press. If your textbook does not have a sufficient section on expertise to aid you in task 3, then this volume of recent articles into this area will be an asset to your wider reading.

NEWELL, A., & SIMON, H. A. (1972). *Human problem solving*. Englewood Cliffs, NJ: Prentice-Hall. This provides an in-depth discussion by one of the key thinkers in this field.

2.13

judgements and decision making

Core Areas

- Anticipated regret
- Availability heuristic
- Base rate information
- Bayes' theorem
- Conjunction fallacy
- Decision making
- Framing
- Judgements
- Loss aversion
- Omission bias
- Perceived justification
- Posterior odds
- Prior odds
- Representativeness heuristic
- Sunk-cost effect
- Utility theory

Learning Outcomes

By the end of this chapter you should be able to;

- define the key terms and theories involved in this topic;
- understand that judgements are made on the basis of probabilities, including the use of prior and posterior odds and base rate information, the representativeness and availability heuristics;
- use the set tasks to research the supporting evidence for these concepts and thus evaluate their usefulness; and
- understand that decision making can be accounted for by utility theory but affected by loss aversion, the sunk-cost effect, framing, perceived justification, anticipated regret and self-esteem.

Running Themes

- Ecological validity
- Experimental cognitive psychology
- Gestalt psychology
- Rehearsal
- Schema
- Semantics

Introduction

Judgements involve looking at the conclusions we draw on the basis of available evidence and knowledge, and is usually concerned with statistical judgements.

Decision making involves making significant and personal choices when provided with options, in other words, making a cost–benefit analysis.

Decision making is more of a personal process than a mathematical calculation.

Key Thinkers

Bayes' theorem, see Eysenck & Keane (2000, p. 476)

To make any judgement we need to take into account the probability of the two beliefs/hypotheses in a given situation before new data was obtained (*prior odds*) and the relative probability of obtaining the data under each hypothesis (*posterior odds*). We then evaluate the probability of observing the data if hypothesis A and B are correct. Thus, judgements are made on the basis of the probability of outcomes subsequent to new evidence.

However, it was found that people do not make much use of prior odds/base rate information, defined by Koehler (1996) as 'the relative frequency with which an event occurs or an attribute is present in the population' (quoted in Eysenck & Keane, 2000, p. 477). Although, according to Eysenck & Keane specific factors can partially reverse this, for example, if there is causal relevance.

Tversky & Kahneman's representativeness heuristic (1973)

Hill (2001, p. 137) defines the representativeness heuristic as 'estimating the probability of a particular sample of events based on their similarity to characteristics we feel are typical of the whole category population of those events'. So, judgements are made on the probability of perceived trends. However, if base rate information is ignored, or principles of representativeness (for example, the representativeness of small samples) are not followed, then incorrect judgements are made. The *conjunction fallacy*, that is, the incorrect belief that a conjunction of two events is more likely than one of the two events, then operates, although there is some inconsistent evidence about its existence.

Tversky & Kahneman's availability heuristic (1974)

As familiar/recent events are more readily available to memory, then they are seen as more probable; therefore, estimates of probability are dependent on past recollections and retrieval of information from LTM. Thus, it is based partly on occurrence, with a correlation between frequency and subsequent judgement on the basis of the perceived probability.

Rottenstreich & Tversky (1997)

Developed Tversky & Koehler's theory (1994) and went on to argue that judgements are made on the basis of how explicitly an event is described – with an explicit event, judged as more probable. This is because it specifically focuses attention on certain aspects of the event, and we know from research that memory can be selective in recalling facts unless cues or information are provided (adapted from the reasons given by Eysenck & Keane, 2000, p. 481). Evidence for this is provided by Johnson, Hashtroudi & Lindsay (1993), where participants predicted they would pay a higher price for a hypothetical insurance policy if terms were explicit.

REMEMBER

Judgements are the result of:

➢ the probability of outcomes subsequent to new evidence
➢ the probability of perceived trends
➢ estimates of probability based on past recollections and retrieval of information from LTM
➢ how explicitly an event is described – with an explicit event judged as more probable.

Handy Hints for Evaluating the Work of Key Thinkers

- Koehler (1996) believed that base rate information, though not ignored, is not accepted as much as it should be.
- The ecological validity of studies into the use of such information is questionable and due to the order in which information was presented in laboratory studies, including the way probabilitiies are phrased, whereas in real-life situations base rate information may be unavailable or of limited use.
- Gigerenzer (1996) suggested the following limits:

  (a) The concepts of heuristics are too general and there is not enough detail provided about the exact processes involved, where and when they are employed.
  (b) The work is too laboratory-based, since judgements are not made on statistical principles and probability in the real world.
  (c) Confounding variables can account for the findings and misunderstanding of the questions asked, so again difficulties with applying such research in the laboratory arises where research is prone to experimenter effects.
  (d) Probability can't be used to make judgements about unique events, since these are one off occurrences not prone to using information about prior frequencies.

Approaches to Decision Making

Utility theory (Neumann & Morgenstern, 1947)

When making decisions we try to assess the value of an outcome or 'maximise utility'. To do this we weigh up the probability of a given outcome and the utility (value) of the outcome. Hence:

$$\text{Expected utility} = (\text{probability of a given outcome}) \times (\text{utility of the outcome})$$

> In other words it is a kind of cost–benefit analysis, but choices can also be affected by loss aversion and the sunk-cost effect, framing, perceived justification, anticipated regret and self-esteem.

Loss aversion

When making decisions we tend to focus more on what we could lose rather than what we could gain. This was supported by Kahneman & Tversky (1984) who found that if people were given the chance of winning $10 or $20 if a tossed coin came up heads, but losing $10 if it was tails, then they refused the bet because their primary focus in their decision making was how much they might lose.

Sunk-cost effect

Additional resources are used to further support a previous commitment (as in the saying 'throwing good money after bad').

Framing

Presents particular problems when testing decision making, because it is concerned with the phrasing or presentation of a problem.

Perceived justification

Decisions are made on the basis to which they can be justified. Tversky & Shafir (1992) found that of three exam groups who could go to Hawaii for a cheap holiday, those who knew they had either passed or failed could justify going because they felt they were justified in either celebrating or recovering. On the other hand, the group whose results were unknown could not justify it to themselves and were more likely to stay and await their grade.

Anticipated regret

If we believe we will regret a decision, then we are likely to avoid that decision even though it might have been a good one to make. Therefore, actions may be avoided to prevent such regret (*omission bias* – Baron, 1997).

Self-esteem

Understandably, people with low self-esteem are more concerned with how they will be evaluated by others and are therefore concerned with making the 'right decision'. As a result, they are much less likely to take risks when making decisions than people who are confident and have high self-esteem.

REMEMBER

Decision making is influenced by:

- ➢ the probability of a given outcome versus the value of it
- ➢ the potential losses
- ➢ the phrasing or presentation of a problem
- ➢ the justification that can be made for it
- ➢ the anticipated regret
- ➢ the level of self-esteem.

You must note, however, that not all decision making is flawed.

Tasks

1 Think about a decision you have recently made, for example, which university/course to choose. List the reasons why you made your decision. Now look back on the theories presented in this chapter and discuss or record how they relate to judgements/decisions you made.

2 Read pp. 476–479 in Eysenck & Keane (2000) and record the relevant supporting studies for each of the following:

- Bayes' theorem – Tversky & Kahneman (1980)
- Base rate information – Tversky & Kahneman (1980)
- Real-world research – Christensen-Szalanski & Bushyhead (1981)
- Representativeness heuristic – Kahneman & Tversky (1973)

Once you have a record of them you then need to specifically outline exactly how they provide support.

3 Use evidence to indicate how the 'Asian disease problem' used in the study by Tversky & Kahneman (1987) provides evidence for the role of framing in decision making.

"Describe and evaluate research (theories and/or studies) into Judgement and decision-making processes"

This title gives you the option of discussing any of the material in this chapter; however, it is critical that you attempt to be selective, since you will otherwise end up covering a lot of information in very little depth. Alternatively, you need to focus on a few of the key theories. Then, as the question asks, initially describe the relevant theory, but, more importantly, use research studies to indicate support for these. This will require you to engage in discussion about how the studies provide support for the processes you have outlined. In order to present a balanced view, it is then vital that you also address the problematic areas that have arisen in such work, including a focus on the research methods and validity.

Common Pitfalls

- *This chapter has simply presented the basic work of the key thinkers and theorists involved in decision-making and judgements. You will, however, need to complete the tasks in order to support such description with analysis, therefore focusing on which material supports and criticises the outlined work, and, more importantly, why.*
- *Ensure you are clear about the terms involved in this topic, especially with regard to those that belong to a discussion on judgements and those that belong to a discussion on decision making.*
- *Since there are many studies by the same psychologists (for example, Tversky & Kahneman), it is essential that you do not confuse them. It may help to draw up a simple list of each of the studies – giving each one a title or a few bullet points to act as reminders.*

Textbook guide

KAHNEMAN, D., & TVERSKY, D. (1996). On the reality of cognitive illusions. *Psychological Review, 103*, 582–591. This will aid your evaluation of research in this field, as it is a discussion on the strengths and weaknesses of Kahneman & Tversky's work.

LUCE, L. L. (1996). When four distinct ways to measure utility are the same. *Journal of Mathematical Psychology, 40,* 297–317. This provides an up-to-date discussion on utility theory.

GIGERENZER, G., TODD, P. M., & THE ABC RESEARCH GROUP (1999). *Simple heuristics that make us smart.* Oxford: Oxford University Press. More information on contemporary research into this important field.

2.14

reasoning and deduction

Core Areas

- Abstract rule theory
- Affirmation of the consequence
- Deductive reasoning
- Denial of the antecedent
- Domain-specific theories
- Heuristic and bias accounts
- Inductive reasoning
- Mental models
- Modus ponens
- Modus tollens
- Pragmatic reasoning schemata
- Probabilistic theory
- Social contract schemata

Learning Outcomes

By the end of this chapter you should be able to:

- define the key terms outlined above;
- be able to describe the explanations psychologists have offered for reasoning, including the abstract rule theory, mental models, domain-specific theories, heuristic and bias accounts and probabilistic theory;
- understand the key ideas central to deductive reasoning, that is, modus ponens, modus tollens, affirmation of the consequence and denial of the antecedent;
- evaluate each of these.

Running Themes

- Bottom-up processing.
- Cognitive neuropsychology
- Cognitive neuroscience
- Ecological validity
- Experimental cognitive psychology
- Schema
- Semantics
- Top-down processing

Introduction

There are two types of reasoning:

- **Deductive reasoning:** where a logical conclusion is made following a statement that is usually true. It is based on what is called the 'propositional calculus', which involves logical operators, for example, not, and, or, if ... then, if and only if. Such logic put more simply involves making decisions where 'if A happens then conclusion B can be drawn'. Truth tables are used to work out if a statement is true or false so that reasoning can take place and to provide a guide on what inferences are correct or incorrect according to logic.
- There are four key ideas central to deductive reasoning: **modus ponens, modus tollens, affirmation of the consequence** and **denial of the antecedent**.

All of these can be considered under the conditional inference of 'if A then B'. For example, 'if there is a sale in the shop (A) then I will buy clothes (B)'. For modus ponens, if A is true (there is a sale in the shop), then B is also true (I will buy clothes). For modus tollens, if B is false (that is, I have *not* bought clothes), then A is also false (that is, there was no sale in the shop). Affirmation of the consequence is a common mistake where people assume that because B is true (I have bought clothes), then A must be true (there was a sale); however, since there are a number of reasons why people buy clothes, it is not valid to claim there was a sale. Another similar mistake in reasoning is the denial of the antecedent. Here, A is false (there is *no* sale) and people commonly assume that this means B (I have *not* bought clothes) is false as well. However, as stated above, the absence of a sale does not preclude people from buying clothes, which means again that no firm conclusion can be made. Marcus and Rips (1979) found that nearly all people make the valid modus ponens inference, half of people make the correct modus tollens inference while up to 70% of people make the incorrect affirmation of consequence and denial of the antecedent. This is important, as any model of deductive reasoning should be able to explain this.

- **Inductive reasoning**: general conclusions drawn about particular statements, often based on previous experience. For example, 'Every time I have kicked a ball in the air it has come back down.' So if I kick a ball up in the air again, inductive reasoning would suggest that it is logical to predict that it will come back down again.

Incorrect inferences can also be affected by context.

Key Theories

Braine & O'Brien's abstract rule theory (1991)

Reason is determined by mental logic and abstract, content-free rules are used. Mistakes are made because the original problem either is misunderstood or is difficult and exceeds working memory capability. Direct reasoning involves the use of schemas, which help form conclusions, but indirect reasoning has to rely on other systems (such as domain-specific ones – see below), which may lead to response bias. Errors can be made comprehending or representing the problem, actioning the appropriate schemas or inadequate and incorrect processing.

Mental models

These are constructed on the basis of possibilities and a conclusion is reached when these are verified. No other examples can be sought. Again, if a large number of models have to be considered before a conclusion is drawn, then working memory capability may be exceeded, thus leading to mistakes being made. These tend to arise specifically when different interpretations are made of an assumption and therefore fail to draw upon the most helpful mental model in their reasoning process.

Domain-specific theories

Initially, an overall mechanism controls reasoning (such as those above), but it then becomes a more specific process because a second mechanism acknowledges the importance of domain-specific schemas. In other words, previous knowledge and experience aids reasoning in different situations. Pragmatic reasoning schemata are used to reason conclusions about everyday situations. Although these can potentially apply to a wide range of situations, in practice they are limited by goals and general relationships between things. For example, obligation schemata aid reasoning of a situation where you feel obliged to do something. Social contract theory (Cosmides, 1989) believes that domain-specific rules exist in accordance within the Darwinian theory of evolution and that reasoning rests on the idea that ensures goal achievement in the social context to enhance survival.

Heuristic and bias accounts

Most people are inherently logical but biases/heuristics override this.

Oaksford & Chater's probabilistic theory (1994, 1995, 1996)

Reasoning is simply based on the probability of gaining information whilst reducing uncertainty.

REMEMBER

Theories of Reasoning

➢ Reason is determined by mental logic and abstract, content-free rules are used. Mistakes are made because the original problem either is misunderstood or is difficult and exceeds working memory capability.

> ➢ Mental models are constructed on the basis of possibilities and a conclusion is reached when these are verified. No other examples can be sought.
> ➢ Previous knowledge and experience aids reasoning in different situations.
> ➢ Most people are inherently logical but biases/heuristics override this.
> ➢ Reasoning is simply based on the probability of gaining information whilst reducing uncertainty.

Handy Hints for Evaluating Key Theories of Reasoning

- When tested empirically the abstract theory has some supporting evidence, as the difficulty of a problem was correlated with mistakes made. However, the theory would need to be considerably expanded upon in terms of how people actually comprehend problems and the interaction with other factors, such as context, in relation to this. A similar criticism can also be applied to the mental model accounts.
- The mental model also fails in the notion that any number of models can be used to reason a single problem, since it undermines the very prediction that these are constructed on the basis of possibilities and a conclusion is reached when these are verified, and no other examples can be sought. Indeed, there is not even specification of how counterexamples are validated, which is a key assumption of the theory.
- Domain-specific theories do not fully account for all types of reasoning or the alternatives that might be used when these are not in operation. The exact mechanisms behind social contract and pragmatic reasoning are unaccounted for, certainly in terms of how such schemata are originally derived.
- Probabilistic theory usefully links the ideas on reasoning with those on judgements and decision making, which is useful because they could be viewed as integral processes. However it still needs to be tested more extensively.
- The general difficulty with all of these theories is that reasoning processes are hard to test empirically, and that obviously poses difficulties for applying them within a wider context.

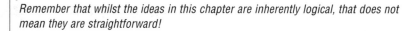

> *Remember that whilst the ideas in this chapter are inherently logical, that does not mean they are straightforward!*

Tasks

1 Use your textbooks to look up Watson's selection task. Using the headings 'aim, procedure, findings', identify what this task predicts and how it was carried out.

2 Now take each of the theories of reasoning outlined below and write a paragraph on each one, showing how they explain the findings on selection task.

"Discuss how psychologists explain reasoning."

To start any discussion on reasoning it is important that you outline the types of reasoning that have been identified (deductive and inductive) and then proceed to describe the theoretical explanations offered for this process, as outlined in this chapter. You will then need to develop your research from the tasks above and the evaluative points made in this chapter to outline supporting psychological examples of each type of reasoning, which you will have noted often contain specific examples rather than general studies. Many of the key criticisms have been stated above, but again it is not sufficient just to simply copy this into an essay format. Instead, you will need to expand on the exact aspects of the theories they support and criticise, so that the examiner can see your depth of understanding.

Common Pitfalls

- *It is common for students to try and ignore the logical principles and importance of the selection task because of the technical language and mathematical principles involved, which then makes it difficult to truly evaluate the theories. If this applies to you, spend an initial period of time grasping these concepts first.*
- *Evaluation requires you to focus on both the positives and the negatives of the theories.*
- *When looking at tasks set by researchers, ensure that you yourself understand the correct answer to the task, so that you can better understand the mistakes made by the participants.*

Textbook guide

MANKTELOW, K. I. (1999). *Reasoning and thinking*. Hove, UK: Psychology Press. An excellent general text offering broad coverage of this topic.

OAKSFORD, M. R., & CHATER, N. (1994). A rational analysis of the selection task as optimal data selection. *Psychological Review, 101,* 608–631.

OAKSFORD, M. R., & CHATER (1995). Information gain explains relevance which explains the selection task. *Cognition, 57,* 97–108.

OAKSFORD, M. R., & CHATER (1996). Rational explanation of the selection task. *Psychological Review, 103,* 381–391.

Together, the three Oaksford & Chater articles will provide comprehensive coverage of the probabilistic theory.

part three*
study and revision skills

*in collaboration with David McIlroy

3.1

introduction

if you work your way carefully through Part Three you should at the end be better equipped to:

- profit from your lectures;
- benefit from your seminars;
- construct your essays efficiently;
- develop effective revision strategies; and
- respond comprehensively to the pressures of exam situations.

In the sections that lie ahead you will be presented with:

- checklists and bullet points to focus your attention on key issues;
- exercises to help you participate actively in the learning experiences;
- illustrations and analogies to enable you to anchor learning principles in everyday events and experiences;
- worked examples to demonstrate the use of such features as structure, headings and continuity; and
- tips that provide practical advice in nutshell form.

In the exercise that are presented, each student should decide how much effort they would like to invest in each exercise, according to individual preferences and requirements. Some of the points in the exercises will be covered in the text either before or after the exercise. You might prefer to read each section right through before going back to tackle the exercises. Suggested answers are provided in italics after some of the exercises, so avoid these if you prefer to work through the exercises on your own. The aim is to prompt you to reflect on the material, remember what you have read and trigger you to add your own thoughts. Space is provided for you to write your responses down in a few words, or you may prefer to reflect on them within your own mind. However, writing will help you to slow down and digest the material and may also enable you to process the information at a deeper level of learning.

Finally the overall aim of Part Three is to point you to the keys for academic and personal development. The twin emphases of academic development and personal qualities are stressed throughout. By giving attention to these factors you will give yourself the toolkit you will need to excel in your psychology course.

3.2	
how to get the most out of your lectures	

This section will enable you to:

- make the most of your lecture notes
- prepare your mind for new terms
- develop an independent approach to learning
- write efficient summary notes from lectures
- take the initiative in building on your lectures

Keeping in Context

According to higher educational commentators and advisors, best quality learning is facilitated when it is set within an overall learning context. It should be the responsibility of your tutors to provide a context for you to learn in, but it is your responsibility to see the overall context, and you can do this even before your first lecture begins. Such a panoramic view can be achieved by becoming familiar with the outline content of both psychology as a subject and the entire study programme. Before you go into each lecture you should briefly remind yourself of where it fits into the overall scheme of things. Think, for example, of how more confident you feel when you move into a new city (for example, to attend university) once you become familiar with your bearings, such as where you live in relation to college, shops, stores, buses, trains, places of entertainment and so on.

> *The same principle applies to your course – find your way around your study programme and locate the position of each lecture within this overall framework.*

Use of Lecture Notes

It is always beneficial to do some preliminary reading before you enter a lecture. If lecture notes are provided in advance (for example, electronically), then print these out, read over them and bring them with you to the lecture. You can insert question marks on issues where you will need further clarification. Some lecturers prefer to provide full notes, some prefer to make skeleton outlines available and some prefer to issue no notes at all! If notes are provided, take full advantage and supplement these with your own notes as you listen. In a later section on memory techniques you will see that humans possess ability for 're-learning savings' – that is it is easier to learn material the second time round, as it is evident that we have a capacity to hold residual memory deposits. So some basic preparation will equip you with a great advantage; you will be able to 'tune in' and think more clearly about the lecture than you would have done with the preliminary work.

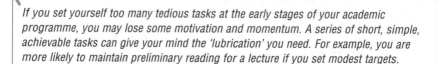

If you set yourself too many tedious tasks at the early stages of your academic programme, you may lose some motivation and momentum. A series of short, simple, achievable tasks can give your mind the 'lubrication' you need. For example, you are more likely to maintain preliminary reading for a lecture if you set modest targets.

Mastering Technical Terms

Let us assume that in an early lecture you are introduced to a series of new terms such as 'paradigm', 'empirical' and 'ecological validity'. If you are hearing these and other terms for the first time, you could end up with a headache! New words can be threatening, especially if you have to face a string of them in one lecture. The uncertainty about the new terms may impair your ability to benefit fully from the lecture and therefore hinder the quality of your learning. Psychology requires technical terms, and the use of them is unavoidable. However, when you have heard a term a number of times it will not seem as daunting as it initially was. It is claimed that individuals may have particular strengths in the scope of their vocabulary. Some people may have a good recognition vocabulary – they immediately know what a word means when they read it or hear it in context. Others have a good command of language when they speak – they have an ability to recall words freely. Still others are more fluent in recall when they write – words seem to flow rapidly for them when they engage in the dynamics of writing. You can work at developing all three approaches in your course, and the checklist below the next paragraph may be of some help in mastering and marshalling the terms you hear in lectures.

In terms of learning new words, it will be very useful if you can first try to work out what they mean from their context when you first encounter them. You might be much better at this than you imagine, especially if there is only one word in the sentence that you do not understand. It would also be very useful if you could obtain a small indexed notebook and use this to build up your own glossary of terms. In this way you could include a definition of a word, an example of its use, where it fits into a theory and any practical application of it.

Checklist: Mastering terms used in your lectures

✓ Read lecture notes before the lectures and list any unfamiliar terms.

✓ Read over the listed terms until you are familiar with their sound.

✓ Try to work out meanings of terms from their context.

✓ Do not suspend learning the meaning of a term indefinitely.

✓ Write out a sentence that includes the new word (do this for each word).

✓ Meet with other students and test each other with the technical terms.

✓ Jot down new words you hear in lectures and check out the meaning soon afterwards.

Your confidence will greatly increase when you begin to follow the flow of arguments that contain technical terms, and more especially when you can freely use the terms yourself in speaking and writing.

Developing Independent Study

In the current educational ethos there are the twin aims of cultivating teamwork/group activities and independent learning. There is not necessarily a conflict between the two, as they should complement each other. For example, if you are committed to independent learning you have more to offer other students when you work in small groups, and you will also be prompted to follow up on the leads given by them. Furthermore, the guidelines given to you in lectures are designed to lead you into deeper independent study. The issues raised in lectures are pointers to provide direction and structure for your extended personal pursuit. Your aim should invariably be to build on what you are given, and you should never think of merely returning the bare bones of the lecture material in a course work essay or exam.

> *It is always very refreshing to a marker to be given work from a student that contains recent studies that the examiner had not previously encountered.*

Note-taking strategy

Note-taking in lectures is an art that you will perfect only with practise and by trial and error. Each student should find the formula that works best for him or her. What works for one does not necessarily work for the other. Some students can write more quickly than others, some are better at shorthand than others and some are better at deciphering their own scrawl! The problem will always be to try to find a balance between concentrating beneficially on what you hear with making sufficient notes that will enable you to comprehend later what you have heard. You should not, however, become frustrated by the fact that will not understand or remember immediately everything you have heard.

> *By being present at a lecture, and by making some attempt to attend to what you hear, you will already have a substantial advantage over those students who do not attend.*

Checklist: Note-taking in lectures

✓ Develop the note-taking strategy that works best for you.
✓ Work at finding a balance between listening and writing.
✓ Make some use of optimal shorthand (for example, a few key words may summarise a story).
✓ Too much writing may impair the flow of the lecture for you.
✓ Too much writing may impair the quality of your notes.
✓ Some limited notes are better than none.
✓ Good note-taking may facilitate deeper processing of information.

✓ It is essential to 'tidy up' notes as soon as possible after a lecture.

✓ Reading over notes soon after lectures will consolidate your learning.

Developing the Lecture

Some educationalists have criticised the value of lectures because they allege that these are a mode of merely 'passive learning'. This can certainly be an accurate conclusion to arrive at (that is, if students approach lectures in the wrong way) and lecturers can work to devise ways of making lectures more interactive. For example, they can make use of interactive handouts or by posing questions during the lecture and giving time out for students to reflect on these. Other possibilities are short discussions at given junctures in the lecture or use of small groups within the session. As a student you do not have to enter a lecture in passive mode, and you can ensure that you are not merely a passive recipient of information by taking steps to develop the lecture yourself. A list of suggestions is presented below to help you take the initiative in developing the lecture content.

Checklist: Avoid lecture being a passive experience

✓ Try to interact with the lecture material by asking questions.

✓ Highlight points that you would like to develop in personal study.

✓ Trace connections between the lecture and other parts of your study programme.

✓ Bring together notes from the lecture and other sources.

✓ Restructure the lecture outline into your own preferred format.

✓ Think of ways in which aspects of the lecture material can be applied.

✓ Design ways in which aspects of the lecture material can be illustrated.

✓ If the lecturer invites questions, make a note of all the questions asked.

✓ Follow up on issues of interest that have arisen from the lecture.

> *You can contribute to this active involvement in a lecture by engaging with the material before, during and after it is delivered.*

Summarise (and/or add) some factors that would help you fully to capitalise on the benefits of a lecture.

....

....

....

....

| 3.3 | |
| how to make the most of seminars | |

This section will enable you to:

- be aware of the value of seminars
- focus on links to learning
- recognise qualities you can use repeatedly
- manage potential problems in seminars
- prepare yourself adequately for seminars

Not to be Underestimated

Seminars are often optional in a degree programme and sometimes poorly attended because they are underestimated. Some students may be convinced that the lecture is the truly authoritative way to receive quality information. Undoubtedly, lectures play an important role in an academic programme, but seminars have a unique contribution to learning that will complement lectures. Other students may feel that their time would be better spent in personal study. Again, private study is unquestionably essential for personal learning and development; nevertheless you will diminish your learning experience if you neglect seminars. If seminars were to be removed from academic programmes, then something really important would be lost.

Checklist: Some useful features of seminars

✓ Can identify problems that you had not thought of
✓ Can clear up confusing issues
✓ Allows you to ask questions and make comments
✓ Can help you develop friendships and teamwork
✓ Enables you to refresh and consolidate your knowledge
✓ Can help you sharpen motivation and redirect study efforts

An Asset to Complement Other Learning Activities

In higher education at present there is emphasis on variety – variety in delivery, learning experience, learning styles and assessment methods. The seminar is deemed to hold an important place within the overall scheme of teaching, learning and assessment. In some programmes the seminars are directly linked to the assessment task. Whether or not they have such a place in your course, they will provide you with a unique opportunity to learn and develop.

In a seminar you will hear a variety of contributions, and different perspectives and emphases. You will have the chance to interrupt and the experience of being interrupted! You will also learn that you can get things wrong and still survive! It is often the case that when one student admits that they did not know an important piece of information, other students quickly follow on to the same admission in the wake of this. If you can learn to ask questions and not feel stupid, then seminars will give you an asset for learning and a lifelong educational quality.

Creating the Right Climate in Seminars

It has been said that we have been given only one mouth to talk, but two ears to listen. One potential problem with seminars is that some students may take a while to learn this lesson, and other students may have to help hasten them on the way (graciously but firmly!). In lectures your main role is to listen and take notes, but in seminars there is the challenge to strike the balance between listening and speaking. It is important to make a beginning in speaking even if it is just to repeat something that you agree with. You can also learn to disagree in an agreeable way. For example, you can raise a question against what someone else has said and pose this in a good tone, for example, 'If that is the case, does that not mean that…' In addition, it is perfectly possible to disagree with others by avoiding personal attacks, such as, 'That was a really stupid thing to say', or 'I thought you knew better than that', or 'I'm surprised that you don't know that by now.' Educationalists say that it is important to have the right climate to learn in, and the avoidance of unnecessary conflict will foster such a climate.

EXERCISE

Suggest what can be done to reach agreement (set ground rules) that would help keep seminars running smoothly and harmoniously.

....

....

....

....

Some suggestions are: Appoint someone to guide and control the discussion, invite individuals to prepare in advance to make a contribution, hand out agreed discussion questions at some point prior to the seminar, stress at the beginning that no one should monopolise the discussion and emphasise that there must be no personal attacks on any individual (state clearly what this means). Also you could invite and encourage quieter students to participate and assure each person that their contribution is valued.

Links in Learning and Transferable Skills

An important principle in learning to progress from shallow to deep learning is developing the capacity to make connecting links between themes or topics and across subjects. This also applies to the various learning activities, such as lectures, seminars, fieldwork, computer searches and private study. Another factor to think about is, 'What skills can I develop, or improve on, from seminars that I can use across my study programme?' A couple of examples of key skills are the ability to communicate and the capacity to work within a team. These are skills that you will be able to use at various points in your course (transferable), but you are not likely to develop them within the formal setting of a lecture.

EXERCISE

Write out or think about (a) three things that give seminars value, and (b) three useful skills that you can develop in seminars.

(a)

✓ ....

✓ ....

✓ ....

(b)

✓ ....

✓ ....

In the above exercises, for (a) you could have: variety of contributors, flexibility to spend more time on problematic issues and agreed agenda settled at the beginning of the seminar. For (b) you could have: communication, conflict resolution and teamwork.

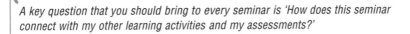

A key question that you should bring to every seminar is 'How does this seminar connect with my other learning activities and my assessments?'

An Opportunity to Contribute

If you have never made a contribution to a seminar before, you may need something to use as an 'icebreaker'. It does not matter if your first contribution is only a sentence or two – the important thing is to make a start. One way to do this is to make brief notes as others contribute, and whilst doing this a question or two might arise in your mind. If your first contribution is a question, that is a good start. Or it may be that you will be able to point out some connection between what others have said, or identify conflicting opinions that need to be resolved. If you have already begun making contributions, it is important that you keep the momentum going, and do not allow yourself to lapse back into the safe cocoon of shyness.

EXERCISE

Suggest how you might resolve some of the following problems that might hinder you from making a contribution to seminars.

- One student who dominates and monopolises the discussion.

- Someone else has already said what you really want to say.

- Fear that someone else will correct you and make you feel stupid.

- Feel that your contribution might be seen as short and shallow.

- A previous negative experience puts you off making any more contributions.

Strategies for Benefiting from Your Seminar Experience

If you are required to bring a presentation to your seminar, you might want to consult a full chapter on presentations in a complementary study guide (McIlroy, 2003). Alternatively, you may be content with the summary bullet points presented at the end of this section. In order to benefit from discussions in seminars (the focus of this section), some useful summary nutshells are now presented as a checklist.

Checklist: How to benefit from seminars

✓ Do some preparatory reading.
✓ Familiarise yourself with the main ideas to be addressed.
✓ Make notes during the seminar.
✓ Make some verbal contribution, even a question.

- ✓ Remind yourself of the skills you can develop.
- ✓ Trace learning links from the seminar to other subjects/topics on your programme.
- ✓ Make brief bullet points on what you should follow up on.
- ✓ Read over your notes as soon as possible after the seminar.
- ✓ Continue discussion with fellow students after the seminar has ended.

If required to give a presentation:

- ✓ Have a practice run with friends.
- ✓ If using visuals, do not obstruct them.
- ✓ Check out beforehand that all equipment works.
- ✓ Space out points clearly on visuals (large and legible).
- ✓ Time talk by visuals (for example, 5 slides by 15-minute talk = 3 minutes per slide).
- ✓ Make sure your talk synchronises with the slide on view at any given point.
- ✓ Project your voice so that all in the room can hear.
- ✓ Inflect your voice and do not stand motionless.
- ✓ Spread eye contact around audience.
- ✓ Avoid twin extremes of fixed gaze at individuals and never looking at anyone.
- ✓ Better to fall a little short of time allocation than run over it.
- ✓ Be selective in what you choose to present.
- ✓ Map out where you are going and summarise main points at the end.

3.4	
essay writing tips	

This section will enable you to:

- engage quickly with the main arguments
- channel your passions constructively
- note your main arguments in an outline

- find and focus on your central topic questions
- weave quotations into your essay

Getting into the Flow

In essay writing, one of your first aims should be to get your mind active and engaged with your subject. Tennis players like to go out onto the court and hit the ball back and forth just before the competitive match begins. This allows them to judge the bounce of the ball, feel its weight against their racket, get used to the height of the net, the parameters of the court and other factors such as temperature, light, sun and the crowd. In the same way you can 'warm up' for your essay by tossing the ideas to and fro within your head before you begin to write. This will allow you to think within the framework of your topic, and this will be especially important if you are coming to the subject for the first time.

The Tributary Principle

A tributary is a stream that runs into a main river as it wends its way to the sea. Similarly, in an essay you should ensure that every idea you introduce is moving towards the overall theme you are addressing. Your idea might, of course, be relevant to a subheading that is in turn relevant to a main heading. Every idea you introduce is to be a 'feeder' into the flowing theme. In addition to tributaries, there can also be 'distributaries', which are streams that flow away from the river. In an essay these would represent the ideas that run away from the main stream of thought and leave the reader trying to work out what their relevance may have been. It is one thing to have grasped your subject thoroughly, but quite another to convince your reader that this is the case. Your aim should be to build up ideas sentence by sentence and paragraph-by-paragraph, until you have communicated your clear purpose to the reader.

It is important in essay writing that you not only include material that is relevant, but also make the linking statements that show the connection to the reader.

Listing and Linking the Key Concepts

Psychology has central concepts that can sometimes be usefully labelled by a single word. Course textbooks may include a glossary of terms and these provide a direct route to the beginning of efficient mastery of the topic. The central words or terms are the essential raw materials that you will need to build upon. Ensure that you learn the words and their definitions, and that you can go on to link the key words together so that in your learning activities you will add understanding to your basic memory work.

> *It is useful to list your key words under general headings, if that is possible and logical. You may not always see the connections immediately, but when you later come back to a problem that seemed intractable, you will often find that your thinking is much clearer.*

Example: Write an essay on 'Decision Making'

You might decide to draft your outline points in the following manner (or you may prefer to use a mind map approach):

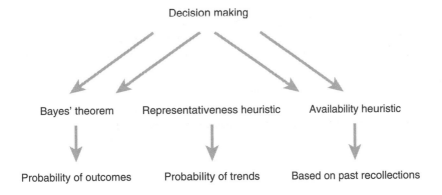

An Adversarial System

In higher education students are required to make the transition from descriptive to critical writing. If you can, think of the critical approach as like a law case that is being conducted where there is both a prosecution and a defence. Your concern should be for objectivity, transparency and fairness. No matter how passionately you may feel about a given cause, you must not allow information to be filtered out because of your personal prejudice. An essay is not to become a crusade for a cause in which the contrary arguments are not addressed in an even-handed manner. This means that you should show awareness that opposite views are held, and you should at least represent these as accurately as possible.

> *Your role as the writer is like that of the judge in that you must ensure that all the evidence is heard, and that nothing will compromise either party.*

Stirring Up Passions

The above points do not, of course, mean that you are not entitled to a personal persuasion or to feel passionately about your subject. On the contrary, such feelings may well be a marked advantage if you can bring them under control and channel them into balanced, effective writing (see example below). Some students may be struggling at the other end of the spectrum – being required to write about a topic that they feel quite indifferent about. As you engage with your topic and toss the ideas around in your mind, you will hopefully find that your interest is stimulated, if only at an intellectual level initially. How strongly you feel about a topic, or how much you are interested in it, may depend on whether you choose the topic yourself or whether it has been given to you as an obligatory assignment.

> *It is important in a large project (such as a dissertation) that you choose a topic for which you can maintain your motivation, momentum and enthusiasm.*

Example: An issue that may stir up passions:

Arguments for and against the view that perception is an innate ability:

For:

- Fantz's visual preference technique (1961) shows that infants prefer discs resembling human faces even from birth.

Against:

- Gibson & Walk's visual cliff study (1960) showed that young infants perceive the danger of depth based on their experience of the world, so perception must be learned.

Structuring an Outline

Whenever you sense a flow of inspiration to write on a given subject, it is essential that you put this into a structure that will allow your inspiration to be communicated clearly. It is a basic principle in all walks of life that structure and order facilitate good communication. Therefore, once you have the flow of inspiration in your essay, you must get this into a structure that will allow the marker to recognise the true quality of your work. For example, you might plan for an introduction, conclusion, three main headings and each of these with several subheadings (see example below). Moreover, you may decide not to include your headings in your final presentation – that is, just use them initially to structure and balance your arguments. Once you have drafted this outline, you can then easily sketch an introduction, and you will have been well prepared for the conclusion when you arrive at that point.

> *A good structure will help you to balance the weight of each of your arguments against each other, and arrange your points in the order that will facilitate the fluent progression of your argument.*

Example: Write an essay that compares and contrasts models of memory

1 *Similarities between theories*

   a. MSM and WMM contain STM store

   b. Look at types of information that can be encoded (for example, visual, acoustic, semantic)

2 *Differences between theories*

    a. Focus on the role of STM

    b. Focus on the role of rehearsal

Finding Major Questions

When you are constructing a draft outline for an essay or project, you should ask what is the major question or questions you wish to address. It would be useful to make a list of all the issues that spring to mind that you might wish to tackle. The ability to design a good question is an art form that should be cultivated, and such questions will allow you to impress your assessor with the quality of your thinking.

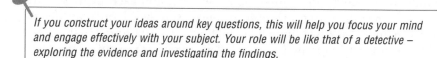

If you construct your ideas around key questions, this will help you focus your mind and engage effectively with your subject. Your role will be like that of a detective – exploring the evidence and investigating the findings.

To illustrate the point, consider the example presented below. If you were asked to write an essay on word/speech recognition, you would need to be aware of not only the theories but also the tips for evaluating the usefulness of such work. For example:

Theories:

- *Liberman et al. (1967) – motor theory.*
- *Marslen-Wilson & Tyler (1980) – cohort theory.*
- *McClelland & Elman (1986) and McClelland (1991) – TRACE model.*
- *McClelland & Rumelhart (1981) – interactive activation model.*

Hints for evaluating them:

- Motor theory can be contradicted by the real-life evidence that is seen in the word recognition of young children who have little experience of motor production in their early years but are nonetheless very astute at recognising words; therefore word recognition must be more complex than the theory would suggest.
- The development of cohort theory was widely accepted as being a more useful version, especially with regard to the greater degree of flexibility it offered

and the stage of contextual processing it presented, although with the flexibility comes less precise specification about its exact operation.

- The TRACE model incorrectly assumed that activation is an immediate response to phonological similarities and there was an overemphasis on the importance of contextual and semantic information. The interactive nature of processing is also questionable and the model cannot account for individual differences in speech patterns, such as timing and speech rates. As with many models focused on language, there is difficulty in generalising the information and results obtained from computer simulations to speech within the real-life context, and as such the theory lacks ecological validity.

Rest Your Case

It should be your aim to give the clear impression that your arguments are not based entirely on hunches, bias, feelings or intuition. In exams and essay questions it is usually assumed (even if not directly specified) that you will appeal to evidence to support your claims. Therefore, when you write your essay you should ensure that it is liberally sprinkled with research evidence. By the time the assessor reaches the end of your work, he or she should be convinced that your conclusions are evidence-based. A fatal flaw to be avoided is to make claims for which you have provided no authoritative source.

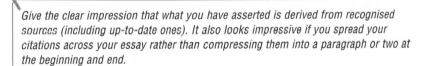

Give the clear impression that what you have asserted is derived from recognised sources (including up-to-date ones). It also looks impressive if you spread your citations across your essay rather than compressing them into a paragraph or two at the beginning and end.

Examples: How to introduce your evidence and sources

According to O'Neil (1999) …
Wilson (2003) has concluded that …
Taylor (2004) found that …
It has been claimed by McKibben (2002) that …
Appleby (2001) asserted that …
A review of the evidence by Lawlor (2004) suggests that …
Findings from a meta-analysis presented by Rea (2003) would indicate that …

It is sensible to vary the expression used so that you are not monotonous and repetitive, and it also aids variety to introduce researchers' names at various places in the sentence (not always at the beginning). It is advisable to choose the expression that is most appropriate – for example, you can make a stronger statement about reviews that have identified recurrent and predominant trends in findings as opposed to one study that appears to run contrary to all the rest.

> *Credit is given for the use of caution and discretion when this is clearly needed.*

Careful Use of Quotations

Although it is desirable to present a good range of cited sources, it is not judicious to present these as 'patchwork quilt' – that is, you just paste together what others have said with little thought for interpretative comment or coherent structure. It is a good general point to aim to avoid very lengthy quotes – short ones can be very effective. Aim also at blending the quotations as naturally as possible into the flow of your sentences. It is good to vary your practices – sometimes use short, direct, brief quotes (cite page number as well as author and year), and at times you can summarise the gist of a quote in your own words. In this case you should cite the author's name and year of publication but leave out quotation marks and page number.

> *Use your quotes and evidence in a manner that demonstrates that you have thought the issues through, and have integrated them in a manner that shows you have been focused and selective in the use of your sources.*

In terms of referencing, practice may vary from one discipline to the next, but some general points that will go a long way in contributing to good practice are:

- If a reference is cited in the text, it must be in the list at the end (and vice versa).
- Names and dates in text should correspond exactly with list in References or Bibliography.
- List of References and Bibliography should be in alphabetical order by the surname (not the initials) of the author or first author.

- Any reference you make in the text should be traceable by the reader (they should clearly be able to identify and trace the source).

A Clearly Defined Introduction

In an introduction to an essay you have the opportunity to define the problem or issue that is being addressed and to set it within context. Resist the temptation to elaborate on any issue at the introductory stage. For example, think of a music composer who throws out hints and suggestions of the motifs that the orchestra will later develop. What he or she does in the introduction is to provide little tasters of what will follow in order to whet the audience's appetite. If you go back to the analogy of the game of tennis, you can think of the introduction as marking out the boundaries of the court in which the game is to be played.

If you leave the introduction and definition of your problem until the end of your writing, you will be better placed to map out the directions that will be taken.

EXERCISE

Look back at the drafted outline on writing an essay on theories of decision making. Design an introduction for that essay in about three or four sentences.

....

....

....

....

Sample answer:
Decision making is the process which involves making significant and personal choices when provided with options, and therefore involves a cost-benefit analysis. Several explanations/theories can be used to explain how such decisions are made including Bayes' theorem, where probability of outcomes are used, and the representativeness and availability heuristics where trends or past recollections help the decision making process.

Conclusion – Adding the Finishing Touches

In the conclusion you should aim to tie your essay together in a clear and coherent manner. It is your last chance to leave an overall impression in your reader's mind. Therefore, you will at this stage want to do justice to your efforts and not sell yourself short. This is your opportunity to identify where the strongest evidence points or where the balance of probability lies. The conclusion to an exam question often has to be written hurriedly under the pressure of time, but with an essay (course work) you have time to reflect on, refine and adjust the content to your satisfaction. It should be your goal to make the conclusion a smooth finish that does justice to the range of content in summary and succinct form. Do not underestimate the value of an effective conclusion. 'Sign off' your essay in a manner that brings closure to the treatment of your subject.

> *The conclusion facilitates the chance to demonstrate where the findings have brought us to date, to highlight the issues that remain unresolved and to point to where future research should take us.*

Top-down and Bottom-up Clarity

An essay gives you the opportunity to refine each sentence and paragraph on your word processor. Each sentence is like a tributary that leads into the stream of the paragraph that in turn leads into the mainstream of the essay. From a 'top-down' perspective (that is, starting at the top with your major outline points), clarity is facilitated by the structure you draft in your outline. You can ensure that the subheadings are appropriately placed under the most relevant main heading, and that both sub and main headings are arranged in logical sequence. From a 'bottom-up' perspective (that is, building up the details that 'flesh out' your main points), you should check that each sentence is a 'feeder' for the predominant concept in a given paragraph. When all this is done, you can check that the transition from one point to the next is smooth rather than abrupt.

Checklist: Summary for essay writing

✓ Before you start, have a 'warm up' by tossing the issues around in your head.

✓ List the major concepts and link them in fluent form.

✓ Design a structure (outline) that will facilitate balance, progression, fluency and clarity.

✓ Pose questions and address these in critical fashion.

✓ Demonstrate that your arguments rest on evidence and spread cited sources across your essay.

✓ Provide an introduction that sets the scene and a conclusion that rounds off the arguments.

EXERCISE

Write (or at least think about) some additional features that would help facilitate good essay writing.

....

....

....

....

....

In the above checklist you could have features such as originality, clarity in sentence and paragraph structure, applied aspects, addressing a subject you feel passionately about and the ability to avoid going off on a tangent.

3.5	
revision hints and tips	

This section will enable you to:

• map out your accumulated material for revision
• choose summary tags to guide your revision
• keep well-organised folders for revision

- make use of effective memory techniques
- develop revision that combines bullet points and in-depth reading
- profit from the benefits of revising with others
- attend to the practical exam details that will help keep panic at bay
- use strategies that keep you task-focused during the exam
- select and apply relevant points from your prepared outlines

The Return Journey

In a return journey you will usually pass by all the same places that you had already passed when you were outward bound. If you had observed the various landmarks on your outward journey, you would be likely to remember them on your return. Similarly, revision is a means to 'revisit' what you have encountered before. Familiarity with your material can help reduce anxiety, inspire confidence and fuel motivation for further learning and good performance.

If you are to capitalise on your revision period, then you must have your materials arranged and at hand for the time when you are ready to make your 'return journey' through your notes.

Start at the Beginning

Strategy for revision should be on your mind from your first lecture at the beginning of your academic semester. You should be like the squirrel that stores up nuts for the winter. Do not waste any lecture, tutorial, seminar, group discussion and so on by letting the material evaporate into thin air. Get into the habit of making a few guidelines for revision after each learning activity. Keep a folder, or file, or little notebook that is reserved for revision and write out the major points that you have learned. By establishing this regular practice you will find that what you have learned becomes consolidated in your mind, and you will also be in a better position to 'import' and 'export' your material both within and across subjects.

If you do this regularly and do not make the task too tedious, you will be amazed at how much useful summary material you have accumulated when revision time comes.

Compile Summary Notes

It would useful and convenient to have a little notebook or cards on which you can write outline summaries that provide you with an overview of your subject at a glance. You could also use 'treasury' tags to hold different batches of cards together whilst still allowing for inserts and re-sorting. Such practical resources can easily be slipped into your pocket or bag and produced when you are on the bus or train or whilst sitting in a traffic jam. They would also be useful if you are standing in a queue or waiting for someone who is not in a rush! A glance over your notes will consolidate your learning and will also activate your mind to think further about your subject. Therefore it would also be useful to make notes of the questions that you would like to think about in greater depth. Your primary task is to get into the habit of constructing outline notes that will be useful for revision, and a worked example is provided below.

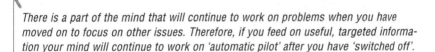

There is a part of the mind that will continue to work on problems when you have moved on to focus on other issues. Therefore, if you feed on useful, targeted information your mind will continue to work on 'automatic pilot' after you have 'switched off'.

Example: Outline revision structure for attention study

1 *Key thinkers/theories*

- Broadbent (1958) – filter theory

- Treisman (1960) – attenuation theory

- Deutsch & Deutsch (1963) – late selection theory

- Johnston & Heinz (1978) – flexible model

2 *Evaluation of these theories*

- Filter theory – seen as being too inflexible and does not account for analysis of the non-shadowed message. It is possible that attention can be switched between channels more easily than Broadbent believed possible.

- Treisman's own work can be supported by his finding that words from a non-attended sentence would be added to the attended sentence if it made it meaningful. However, attenuation theory is complex and the exact role of the attenuator is questionable
- Late selection theory – not supported by experimental evidence. For example, Treisman & Riley (1969) found that target words were better detected in shadowed compared to non-shadowed messages, as this cannot be explained by a process where there is supposed to be equal semantic analysis

Keep Organised Records

People who have a fulfilled career have usually developed the twin skills of time and task management. It is worth pausing to remember that you can use your academic training to prepare for your future career in this respect. Therefore, ensure that you do not fall short of your potential because these qualities have not been cultivated. One important tactic is to keep a folder for each subject and divide this topic by topic. You can keep your topics in the same order in which they are presented in your course lectures. Bind them together in a ring binder or folder and use subject dividers to keep them apart. Make a numbered list of the contents at the beginning of the folder, and list each topic clearly as it marks a new section in your folder. Another important practice is to place all your notes on a given topic within the appropriate section, and don't put off this simple task, do it straight-away. Notes may come from lectures, seminars, tutorials, Internet searches, personal notes and so on. It is also essential when you remove these for consultation that you return them to their 'home' immediately after use.

Academic success has as much to do with good organisation and planning as it has to do with ability. The value of the quality material you have accumulated on your academic programme may be diminished because you have not organised it into an easily retrievable form.

Example: An organised record of a history of romantic relationships

- Physical features my girlfriends/boyfriends have shared or differed in.
- Common and diverse personality characteristics.

- Shared and contrasting interests.
- Frequency of dates with each.
- Places frequented together.
- Contact with both circles of friends.
- Use of humour in our communication.
- Frequency and resolution of conflicts.
- Mutual generosity.
- Courtesy and consideration.
- Punctuality.
- Dress and appearance.

In this fun example, let us imagine that you had five girlfriends/boy friends over the last few years. Each of the five names could be included under all of the above subjects. You could then compare them with each other, looking at what they had in common and how they differed. Moreover, you could think of the ones you liked best and least, then look through your dossier to establish why this might have been. You could also judge who had most and least in common with you and whether you are more attracted to those who differed most from you. The questions open to you can go on and on. The real point here is that you will have gathered a wide variety of material that is organised in such a way that will allow you to use a range of evidence to draw some satisfactory and authoritative conclusions – if that is possible in matters so directly related to the heart!

Use Past Papers

Revision will be very limited if it is confined to memory work. You should by all means read over your revision cards or notebook and keep the picture of the major facts in front of your mind's eye. It is also, however, essential that you become familiar with previous exam papers so that you will have some idea of how the questions are likely to be framed. Therefore, build up a good range of past exam papers (especially recent ones) and add these to your folder. Think of cows and sheep; when they have grazed, they lie down and 'chew the cud'. That is, they regurgitate what they have eaten and take time to digest the food thoroughly.

> If you think over previous exam questions, this will help you not only recall what you have deposited in your memory, but also develop your understanding of the issues. The questions from past exam papers, and further questions that you have developed yourself, will allow you to 'chew the cud'.

Example: Describe and evaluate the working memory model

Immediately you can see that you will require a description and then two lists concerning the support and criticisms and you can begin to work on documenting your reasons under each as below:

Description

- **Central executive:** this is a control system that is modality free and has a limited capacity.
- **Phonological loop:** has an articulatory control system (verbal rehearsal, time-based, inner voice) and a phonological store (speech-based storage system, inner ear).
- **Visuo-spatial scratch pad** ('**inner eye**'): designed for temporary storage and manipulation of spatial and visual information.

Support: Say how each of these supports the WMM

- This model is useful as it deals with active processing and transient storage of information and is involved in all complex cognitive tasks.
- It can explain deficits of STM in brain damaged patients.
- The visuo-spatial scratch pad is useful for geographical orientation and for planning special tasks.
- It is generally accepted that the WMM view of STM as a number of different processing units is better than the MSM view that it is a single unit.
- The idea that any one slave system (for example, the phonological loop) may be involved in the performance of very different tasks is a valuable insight.
- It effectively accounts for our ability to store information briefly whilst at the same time actively processing the material.

Criticisms: Say how each of the following criticises the WMM

- The central executive may not be unitary but may have two or more component systems.
- The role of the central executive is unclear – if it has a limited capacity, what is it?
- One main weakness of the WMM is that *least* is known about the most important component – the central executive. It can apparently carry out an enormous variety of processing activities in different conditions. This makes it difficult to describe its *precise* function, and the idea of a single central executive might be seen as similarly inappropriate as that of a single STM store (Eysenck, 1984)
- Is the WMM really modality free?

- There is a question of whether there is actually a *single* store or if there are separate visual and spatial systems.
- There is also evidence to suggest that verbal and spatial working memory are to some extent separate.

You will have also noticed that the word 'evaluate' is in the question – so your mind must go to work on making judgements. You may decide to work through problems first and then through pleasures, or it may be your preference to compare point by point as you go along. Whatever conclusion you come to may be down to personal subjective preference, but at least you will have worked through all the issues from both standpoints. The lesson is to ensure that part of your revision should include critical thinking as well as memory work.

You cannot think adequately without the raw materials provided by your memory deposits.

Employ Effective Mnemonics (Memory Aids)

The Greek word from which 'mnemonics' is derived refers to a tomb – a structure that is built in memory of a loved one, friend or respected person. 'Mnemonics' can be simply defined as aids to memory – devices that will help you recall information that might otherwise be difficult to retrieve from memory. For example, if you find an old toy in the attic of your house, it may suddenly trigger a flood of childhood memories associated with it. Mnemonics can therefore be thought of as keys that open memory's storehouse.

Visualisation is one technique that can be used to aid memory. For example, the location method is where a familiar journey is visualised and you can 'place' the facts that you wish to remember at various landmarks along the journey, such as a bus stop, a car park, a shop, a store, a bend, a police station, a traffic light and so on. This has the advantage of making an association of the information you have to learn with other material that is already firmly embedded and structured in your memory. Therefore, once the relevant memory is activated, a dynamic 'domino effect' will be triggered. However, there is no reason why you cannot use a whole toolkit of mnemonics. Some examples and illustrations of these are presented below.

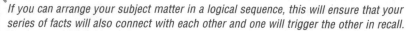

> *If you can arrange your subject matter in a logical sequence, this will ensure that your series of facts will also connect with each other and one will trigger the other in recall.*
>
> *You can use memory devices either at the stage of initial learning or when you later return to consolidate.*

Example: Location method

Visualisation

Turn information into pictures, for example, the problems and pleasures of pets could be envisaged as two tug-of-war teams that pull against each other. You could visualise each player as an argument and have the label written on his or her tee shirt. The war could start with two players and then be joined by another two and so on. In addition, you could compare each player's weight to the strength of each argument. You might also want to make use of colour – your favourite colour for the winning team and the colour you dislike most for the losers!

Alliteration's artful aid

Find a series of words that all begin with the same letter. See the example below related to the experiments of Ebbinghaus.

Peg system

'Hang' information onto a term so that when you hear the term you will remember the ideas connected with it (an umbrella term). For instance, in aggression there are different examples – biological, chronological, sociological and psychological. Under biological you could remember 'psychodynamic' and 'ethological'.

Hierarchical system

This is a development of the previous point with higher order, middle order and lower order terms. For example, you could think of the continents of the world (higher order), then group these into the countries under them (middle order). Under countries you could have cities, rivers and mountains (lower order).

Acronyms

Take the first letter of all the key words and make a word from them.

Mind maps

These have become very popular – they allow you to draw lines that stretch out from the central idea and to develop the subsidiary ideas in the same way. It is a little like the pegging and hierarchical methods combined and turned sideways. The method has the advantage of giving you the complete picture at a glance, although they can become a complex work of art!

Rhymes and Chimes

These are words that rhyme and words that end with a similar sound (for example, commemoration, celebration, anticipation). They provide another dimension to memory work by including sound. Memory can be enhanced when information is processed in various modalities, for example, hearing, seeing, speaking, visualising.

A Confidence Booster

At the end of the 19th century, Ebbinghaus and his assistant memorised lists of nonsense words (could not be remembered by being attached to meaning), and then endeavoured to recall these. What they discovered was:

- Some words could be recalled freely from memory, while others appeared to be forgotten.
- Words that could not be recalled were later recognised as belonging to the lists (that is, were not new additions).
- When the lists were jumbled into a different sequence, the experimenters were able to re-jumble them into the original sequence.
- When the words that were 'forgotten' were learned again, the learning process was much easier the second time (that is, there was evidence of re-learning savings).

The four points of this experiment can be remembered by alliteration: Recall, Recognition, Reconstruction and Re-learning savings. This experiment has been described as a confidence booster because it demonstrates that memory is more powerful than is often imagined, especially when we consider that Ebbinghaus and his assistant did not have the advantage of processing the meaning of the words.

Alternate Between Methods

It is not sufficient to present outline points in response to an exam question (although it is better to do this than nothing if you have run out of time in your exam). Your aim should be to put 'meat on the bones' by adding substance, evidence and arguments to your basic points. You should work at finding the balance between the two methods – outline revision cards might be best reserved for short bus journeys, whereas extended reading might be better employed for longer revision slots at home or in the library. Your ultimate goal should be to bring together an effective, working approach that will enable you to face your exam questions comprehensively and confidently.

In revision it is useful to alternate between scanning over your outline points and reading through your notes, articles, chapters and so on in an in-depth manner. Also, the use of different times, places and methods will provide you with the variety that might prevent monotony and facilitate freshness.

Example: Outline for a course on cognitive psychology

Your major outline topics might be:

- Perception
- Attention
- Memory
- Language
- Thinking

This outline would be your overall, bird's-eye view of the course. You could then choose one of the topics and have all your key terms under that. For example, under 'memory' you might have listed: the multi-store model, encoding and retreival processes, the working memory model, episodic and semantic memory, and learning and memory.

If you alternate between memory work and reading, you will soon be able to think through the processes by just looking at your outlines.

Revising with Others

If you can find a few other students to revise with, this will provide another fresh approach to the last stages of your learning. First ensure that others carry their workload and are not merely using the hard work of others as a short cut to success. You should think of group sessions as one of the strings on your violin, but not the only string. This collective approach would allow you to assess your strengths and weaknesses (showing you where you are off track), and to benefit from the resources and insights of others. Before you meet up you can each design some questions for the whole group to address. The group could also go through past exam papers and discuss the points that might provide an effective response to each question. It should not be the aim of the group to provide standard and identical answers for each group member to mimic. Group work is currently deemed to be advantageous by educationalists, and teamwork is held to be a desirable employability quality.

Each individual should aim to use their own style and content whilst drawing on and benefiting from the group's resources.

EXERCISE

Make a list of the advantages and disadvantages of revising in small groups.

Advantages: **Disadvantages:**

1. ....

2. ....

3. ....

4. ....

5. ....

Can the disadvantages be eliminated or at least minimised?

Checklist: Good study habits for revision time

✓ Set a date for the 'official' beginning of revision and prepare for 'revision mode'.

✓ Do not force cramming by leaving revision too late.

✓ Take breaks from revision to avoid saturation.

✓ Indulge in relaxing activities to give your mind a break from pressure.

✓ Minimise or eliminate use of alcohol during the revision season.

✓ Get into a good rhythm of sleep to allow renewal of your mind.

✓ Avoid excessive caffeine, especially at night so that sleep is not disrupted.

✓ Try to adhere to regular eating patterns.

✓ Try to have a brisk walk in fresh air each day (for example, in the park).

✓ Avoid excessive dependence on junk food and snacks.

EXERCISE

Write your own checklist on what to add to the revision process to ensure that it was not just a memory exercise.

....

....

....

....

....

In the above exercise, what you could add to memory work during revision might include: using past exam papers, setting problem-solving tasks; doing drawings to show connections and directions between various concepts; explaining concepts to student friends in joint revision sessions; devising your own mock exam questions.

3.6	
exam tips	

This section will enable you to:

- develop strategies for controlling your nervous energy
- tackle worked examples of time and task management in exams
- attend to the practical details associated with the exam
- stay focused on the exam questions
- link revision outlines to strategy for addressing exam questions

Handling Your Nerves

Exam nerves are not unusual and it has been concluded that test anxiety arises because of the perception that your performance is being evaluated, that the consequences are likely to be serious and that you are working under the pressure of a time restriction. However, it has also been asserted that the activation of the autonomic nervous system is adaptive in that it is designed to prompt us to take action in order to avoid danger. If you focus on the task at hand rather than on feeding a downward negative spiral in your thinking patterns, this will help you to keep your nerves under control. In the run up to your exams, you can practise some simple relaxation techniques that will help you bring stress under control.

It is a very good thing if you can interpret your nervous reactions positively, but the symptoms are more likely to be problematic if you interpret them negatively, pay too much attention to them or allow them to interfere with your exam preparation or performance.

Practices that may help reduce or buffer the effects of exam stress are:

- listening to music
- going for a brisk walk

- simple breathing exercises
- some muscle relaxation
- watching a movie
- enjoying some laughter
- doing some exercise
- relaxing in a bath (with music if preferred).

The best choice is going to be the one (or combination) that works best for you – perhaps to be discovered by trial and error. Some of the above techniques can be practised on the morning of the exam, and even the memory of them can be used just before the exam. For example, you could run over a relaxing tune in your head and have this echo inside you as you enter the exam room. The idea behind all this is, first, stress levels must come down, and second, relaxing thoughts will serve to displace stressful reactions. It has been said that stress is the body's call to take action, but anxiety is a maladaptive response to that call.

It is important to be convinced that your stress levels can come under control, and that you can have a say in this. Do not give anxiety a vacuum to work in.

Time Management with Examples

The all-important matter as you approach an exam is to develop the belief that you can take control over the situation. As you work through the list of issues that you need to address, you will be able to tick them off one by one. One of the issues you will need to be clear about before the exam is the length of time you should allocate to each question. Sometimes this can be quite simple (although it is always necessary to read the rubric carefully), for example, if 2 questions are to be answered in a 2-hour paper, you should allow 1 hour for each question. If it is a 2-hour paper with 1 essay question and 5 shorter answers, you could allow 1 hour for the essay and 12 minutes each for the shorter questions. However, you always need to check out the weighting for the marks on each question, and you will also need to deduct whatever time it takes you to read over the paper and to choose your questions. Work out a time management strategy in the exercise below. More importantly, give yourself some practise on the papers you are likely to face.

Remember to check if the structure of your exam paper is the same as in previous years, and do not forget that excessive time on your 'strongest' question may not compensate for very poor answers to other questions. Also ensure that you read the rubric carefully in the exam.

Working out the division of exam labour by time

1   A 3-hour paper with 4 compulsory questions (equally weighted in marks).

2   A 3-hour paper with 2 essays and 10 short questions (each of the three sections carry one-third of the marks).

3   A 2-hour paper with 2 essay questions and 100 multiple-choice questions (half marks are on the two essays and half marks on the multiple choice section).

Get into the calculating frame of mind and be sure to have the calculations done before starting the exam. Ensure that the structure of the exam has not changed since the last one. Also deduct the time taken to read over the paper in allocating time to each question.

Suggested answers to previous exercise:

1 *This allows 45 minutes for each question (4 questions x 45 minutes = 2 hours). However, if you allow 40 minutes for each question, this will give you 20 minutes (4 questions x 5 minutes) to read over the paper and plan your outlines.*

2 *In this example you can spend 1 hour on each of the 2 major questions, and 1 hour on the 10 short questions. For the 2 major questions you could allow 10 minutes for reading and planning on each, and 50 minutes for writing. In the 10 short questions, you could allow 6 minutes in total for each (10 questions x 6 minutes = 60 minutes). However, if you allow approximately 1 minute reading and planning time, this will allow 5 minutes writing time for each question.*

In this case you have to divide 120 minutes by 3 questions – this allows 40 minutes for each. You could, for example, allow 5 minutes reading/planning time for each essay and 35 minutes for writing (or 10 minutes reading/planning and 30 minutes writing). After you have completed the 2 major questions you are left with 40 minutes to tackle the 100 multiple-choice questions.

You may not be able to achieve total precision in planning time for tasks, but you will have a greater feeling of control and confidence if you have some reference points to guide you.

Task Management with Examples

After you have decided on the questions you wish to address, you then need to plan your answers. Some students prefer to plan all outlines and draft work at the beginning, whilst others prefer to plan and address one answer before proceeding to address the next question. Decide on your strategy before you enter the exam room, and stick to your plan. When you have done your draft outline as rough work, you should allocate an appropriate time for each section. This will prevent you from excessive treatment of some aspects, whilst falling short on other parts. Such careful planning will help you to achieve balance, fluency and symmetry.

Keep awareness of time limitations; this will help you to write succinctly, keep focused on the task and prevent you dressing up your responses with unnecessary padding.

Some students put as much effort into their rough work as they do into their exam essay.

An over-elaborate mind map may give the impression that the essay is little more than a repetition of this detailed structure, and that the quality of the content has suffered because too much time was spent on the plan.

Work the time allocation for the following outline, allowing for 1 hour on the question. Deduct 10 minutes taken at the beginning for choice and planning.

Distinguish between episodic and semantic memory

1   *Episodic memory*

   (a)   Episodic memory involves the storage and retrieval of specific events (including place and time).

   (b)   Support for episodic memory.

   (c)   Criticisms of episodic memory.

2   *Semantic memory*

   (a)   Semantic memory stores information/meaning about the world, including general and abstract facts.

   (b)   Support for semantic memory.

   (c)   Criticisms of semantic memory.

Attend to Practical Details

This short section is designed to remind you of the practical details that should be attended to in preparation for an exam. There are always students who turn up late, or to the wrong venue or for the wrong exam, or do not turn up at all! Check and re-check that you have all the details of each exam correctly noted. What you don't need is to arrive late and then have to tame your panic reactions. The exam season is the time when you should aim to be at your best.

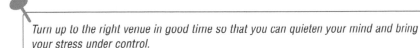

Turn up to the right venue in good time so that you can quieten your mind and bring your stress under control.

Make note of the details in the checklist below and ensure that you have taken control of each one.

Checklist: Practical exam details

✓ Check that you have the correct venue.

✓ Make sure you know how to locate the venue before the exam day.

✓ Ensure that the exam time you have noted is accurate.

✓ Allow sufficient time for your journey and consider the possibility of delays.

✓ Bring an adequate supply of stationery and include spare items such as pens etc.

✓ Bring a watch for your time and task management.

✓ You may need some liquid, such as a small bottle of still water.

✓ You may also need to bring some tissues.

✓ Observe whatever exam regulations your university/college has set in place.

✓ Fill in required personal details before the exam begins.

Control Wandering Thoughts

In a simple study conducted in the 1960s, Ganzer found that students who frequently lifted their heads and looked away from their scripts during exams tended to perform poorly. This makes sense because it implies that the students were taking too much time out when they should have been on task. *One way to fail your exam is to get up and walk out of the test room, but another way is to 'leave' the test room mentally by being preoccupied with distracting thoughts.* The distracting thoughts may be either related to the exam itself or totally irrelevant to it. The net effect of both these forms of intrusion is to distract you from the task at hand and debilitate your test performance. Read over the two lists of distracting thoughts presented below.

Typical test-relevant thoughts (evaluative):

- I wish I had prepared better.
- I wonder what will the examiner think?
- Others are doing better than me.
- What I am writing is nonsense.
- Can't remember important details.

Characteristic test-irrelevant thoughts (non-evaluative):

- Looking forward to this weekend.
- Which video should I watch tonight?

- His remark really annoyed me yesterday!
- I wonder how the game will go on Saturday?
- I wonder if he/she really likes me?

Research has consistently shown that distracting, intrusive thoughts during an exam are more detrimental to performance than stressful symptoms such as sweaty palms, dry mouth, tension, trembling and so on. Moreover, it does not matter whether the distracting thoughts are negative evaluations related to the exam or are totally irrelevant to the exam. The latter may be a form of escape from the stressful situation.

Checklist: Practical suggestions for controlling wandering thoughts

✓ Be aware that this problem is detrimental to performance.

✓ Do not look around to find distractions.

✓ If distracted, write down 'keep focused on task'.

✓ If distracted again, look back at above and continue to do this.

✓ Start to draft rough work as soon as you can.

✓ If you struggle with initial focus, then re-read or elaborate on your rough work.

✓ If you have commenced your essay, re-read your last paragraph (or two).

✓ Do not throw fuel on your distracting thoughts – starve them by re-engaging with the task at hand.

Links to Revision

If you have followed the guidelines given for revision, you will be well equipped with outline plans when you enter the exam room. You may have chosen to use headings and subheadings, mind maps, hierarchical approaches or just a series of simple mnemonics. Whatever method you choose to use, you should be furnished with a series of memory triggers that will open the treasure house door for you once you begin to write.

Although you may have clear templates with a definite structure or framework for organising your material, you will need to be flexible about how this should be applied to your exam questions.

Example: How to use memory triggers

Imagine that perception is one of the topics that you will be examined on. You decide to memorise lists of the topic areas.

Perceptual development

- Fantz's visual preference technique (1961) shows that infants prefer discs resembling human faces even from birth.
- Gibson & Walk's visual cliff study (1960) showed that young infants perceive the danger of depth based on their experience of the world, so perception must be learned.

Organisation

- Aerial perspective
- Familiar size
- Interposition
- Linear perspective
- Motion parallax
- Shading
- Texture
- Convergence
- Accommodation
- Stereopsis

Key thinkers

- Perceptual development – visual preference task (Fantz, 1961).
- Perceptual development – the visual cliff (Gibson & Walk, 1960).
- Perceptual development – enrichment theory (Piaget).
- Perceptual development – differentiation theory.
- Perceptual organisation – Gestalt theory – Law of Pragnanz.
- Colour perception – trichromatic theory (Young-Helmholtz).
- Colour perception – opponent process theory (Hering, 1878).
- Direct, bottom-up theory of perception (Gibson, 1950, 1966, 1979).
- Indirect, constructivist, top-down theory of processing (Gregory, 1972).
- Cyclic theory (Neisser, 1976).

The basic mental template might be these and a few other categories. You know that you will not need every last detail, although you may need to select a few from each category. For example you might be asked to discuss:

- perceptual development;
- if perception is innate or learned;
- perceptual organisation; or
- theories of perception.

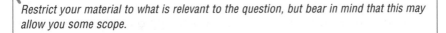

Restrict your material to what is relevant to the question, but bear in mind that this may allow you some scope.

The Art of 'Name Dropping'

In most topics at university you will be required to cite studies as evidence for your arguments and to link these to the names of researchers, scholars or theorists. It will help if you can use the correct dates, or at least the decades, and it is good to demonstrate that you have used contemporary sources and have done some independent work. A marker will have dozens if not hundreds of scripts to work through and they will know if you are just repeating the same phrases from the same sources as everyone else. There is inevitably a certain amount of this that must go on, but there is room for you to add fresh and original touches that demonstrate independence and imagination.

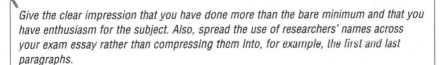

Give the clear impression that you have done more than the bare minimum and that you have enthusiasm for the subject. Also, spread the use of researchers' names across your exam essay rather than compressing them into, for example, the first and last paragraphs.

Flight, Fight or Freeze

As previously noted, the autonomic nervous system (ANS) is activated when danger or apparent danger is imminent. Of course, the threat does not have to be physical, as in the case of an exam, a job interview, a driving test or a television appearance. Indeed, the ANS can be activated even at the anticipation of a future threat. However, the reaction is more likely to be stronger as you enter into the crucial time of testing or challenge. Symptoms may include deep breathing, trembling, headaches, nausea, tension, dry mouth and palpitations. How should we react to these once they have been triggered? A postman might decide to run away from a barking dog and run the risk of being chased and bitten. A second possible response is to freeze on the spot – this might arrest the animal in its tracks, but is no use in an exam situation. In contrast, to fight might not be the best strategy against the dog, but will be more productive in an exam. That is, you are going into the exam room to 'tackle' the questions, and not to run away from the challenge before you.

The final illustration below uses the analogy of archery to demonstrate how you might take control in an exam.

Example: Lessons from archery

- Enter the exam room with a quiver full of arrows – all the points you will need to use.
- Eye up the target board you are to shoot at – choose the exam questions.
- Stand in a good position for balance and vision – prepare your time management.
- Prepare your bow and arrow and take aim at the target – keep focused on the task at hand and do not be sidetracked.
- Pull the string of the bow back to get maximum thrust on the arrow – match your points to the appropriate question.
- Aim to hit the board where the best marks are (bull's-eye or close) – do not be content with the minimum standard, that is, a mere pass.
- Pull out arrows and shoot one after another to gain maximum hits and advantage – do not be content with preparing one or two strong points.
- Make sure your arrows are sharp and the supporting bow and string are firm – choose relevant points and support with evidence.
- Avoid wasted effort by loose and careless shots – do not dress up your essay with unnecessary padding.

EXERCISE

Write your own checklist on the range of combined skills and personal qualities that you will need to be at your best in an exam.

✓ ....

✓ ....

✓ ....

✓ ....

✓ ....

With reference to the above exercise, skills might include such things as critical thinking, time and task management, focus on issues, and quick identification of problems to address. Personal qualities might include factors such as confidence, endurance, resilience and stress control.

3.7	
tips on interpreting essay and exam questions	

This section will enable you to:

- focus on the issues that are relevant and central
- read questions carefully and take account of all the words
- produce a balanced critique in your outline structures
- screen for the key words that will shape your response
- focus on different shades of meaning between 'critique', 'evaluate', 'discuss' and 'compare and contrast'

What Do You See?

The suggested explanation for visual illusions is the inappropriate use of cues – that is, we try to interpret three-dimensional figures in the real world with the limitations of a two-dimensional screen (the retina in the eye). We use cues such as shade, texture, size, background and so on to interpret distance, motion, shape and so forth, and we sometimes use these inappropriately. Another visual practice we engage in is to 'fill in the blanks' or join up the lines (as in the case of the nine lines above – we might assume to be a chair). Our tendency is to impose the nearest similar and familiar template on that which we think we see. The same occurs in the social world – when we are introduced to someone of a different race we may (wrongly) assume certain things about them. The same can also apply to the way you read exam or essay questions. In these cases you are required to 'fill in the blanks', but what you fill in may be the wrong interpretation of the question. This is especially likely if you have primed yourself to expect certain questions to appear in an exam, but it can also happen in course work essays.

Although examiners do not deliberately design questions to trick you or trip you up, they cannot always prevent you from seeing things that were not designed to be there. When one student was asked what the four seasons are, the response given was, 'salt, pepper, mustard and vinegar'. This was not quite what the examiner had in mind!

Go into the exam room, or address the course work essay well prepared, but be flexible enough to structure your learned material around the slant of the question.

A Politician's Answer

Politicians are renowned for refusing to answer questions directly or for evading them through raising other questions. A humorous example is that when a politician was asked, 'is it true that you always answer questions by asking another?', the reply given was, 'Who told you that?' Therefore, make sure that you answer the set question, although there may be other questions that arise out of this for further study that you might want to highlight in your conclusion. As a first principle, you must answer the set question and not another question that you had hoped for in the exam or essay.

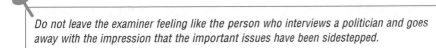

Do not leave the examiner feeling like the person who interviews a politician and goes away with the impression that the important issues have been sidestepped.

Example: Focus on formulating your answer

Discuss the key theories used to explain language production

Directly relevant points:

- Spreading activation theory (Dell, 1986; Dell & O'Seaghdha,1991).
- Anticipation and perseverated errors (Dell et al., 1997).
- WEAVER++ (Word-form Encoding by Activation and VERification) (Levelt, 1989; Levelt et al., 1999a).

Less relevant points:

- Physiology of language production

Although the point listed above may be relevant to language production overall, it is not as directly relevant as the key thinkers in this area. However, it could be mentioned briefly without going off on a tangent.

Be ready to resist the wealth of fascinating material at your disposal that is not directly relevant to your question.

Missing Your Question

A student bitterly complained after an exam that the topic he had revised so thoroughly had not been tested in the exam. The first response to that is that students should always cover enough topics to avoid selling themselves short in the exam – the habit of 'question spotting' is always a risky game to play. However, the reality in the anecdotal example was that the question the student was looking for was there, but he had not seen it. He had expected the question to be couched in certain words and he could not find these when he scanned over the questions in blind panic. Therefore, the simple lesson is: always read over the questions carefully, slowly and thoughtfully. This practice is time well spent.

You can miss the question if you restrict yourself to looking for a set form of words and if you do not read over all the words carefully.

Write it Down

If you write down the question you have chosen to address, and perhaps quietly articulate it with your lips, you are more likely to process fully its true meaning and intent. Think of how easy it is to misunderstand a question that has been put to you verbally because you have misinterpreted the tone or emphasis.

If you read over the question several times, you should be aware of all the key words and will begin to sense the connections between the ideas, and will envisage the possible directions you should take in your response.

Take the following humorous example:

(a)   What is that on the road ahead?
(b)   What is that on the road, a head?

Question (a) calls for the identification of an object (what is that?), but question (b) has converted this into an object that suggests there has been a decapitation! Ensure therefore that you understand the direction the question is pointing you towards so that you do not go off at a tangent. One word in the question that is not properly attended to can throw you completely off track, as in the following example:

(a)   Discuss whether the love of money is the root of all evil.
(b)   Discuss whether money is the root of all evil.

These are two completely different questions, as (a) suggests that the real problem with money is inherent in faulty human use – that is, money itself may not be a bad thing if it is used as a servant and not a master. Whereas (b) may suggest that behind every evil act that has ever been committed, money is likely to have been implicated somewhere in the motive.

Pursue a Critical Approach

In psychology you are expected to write critically rather than merely descriptively, although it may be necessary to use some minimal descriptive substance as the raw material for your debate.

Example: A critical approach

To what extent can forgetting be explained by failures of short-term memory?

Can be explained by failures in STM:

- Trace decay – forgetting as the trace decays over time.
- Displacement – old items of information are replaced by new items.

Cannot be explained by failures in STM:

- Focus on the criticisms of the above approach.
- Use theories that instead suggest it is due to factors in LTM (interference, cue retrieval failure) or emotional factors (flashbulb memories, repression).

Given that the question is about a critical evaluation of the evidence, you would need to address the issues one by one from both standpoints

Analyse the Parts

In an effective sports team the end product is always greater than the sum of the parts. Similarly, a good essay cannot be constructed without reference to the parts. Furthermore, the parts will arise as you break down the question into the components it suggests to you. Although the breaking down of a question into components is not sufficient for an excellent essay, it is a necessary starting point.

To achieve a good response to an exam or essay question, aim to integrate all the individual issues presented in a manner that gives shape and direction to your efforts.

Example

To what extent can forgetting be explained by failures of short- or long-term memory? Two parts to this question are clearly suggested – short-term explanations versus long-term explanations. You are left with the choice of the issues that you wish to address, and you can arrange these in the order you prefer. Your aim should be to ensure that you do not have a lopsided view, and to include both support for and criticisms of both theories.

Give yourself plenty of practise at thinking of questions in this kind of way – both with topics on and not on your course. Topics not on your course that really interest you may be a helpful way to 'break you in' to this critical way of thinking.

Luchins and Learning Sets

In a series of experiments, Luchins (1959) allowed children to learn how to solve a problem that involved pouring water from and into a series of jugs of various sizes and shapes. He then gave them other problems that could be solved by following the same sequence. However, when he later gave them another problem that could be solved through a simpler sequence, they went about solving it through the previously learned procedure. In this case the original approach was more difficult, but it had become so set in the children's minds that they were blinded to the shorter, more direct route.

Example: How much did the wealthy Scottish man leave behind?

The story is told of a wealthy Scottish man who died, and no one in his village knew how much he had left behind. The issue was debated and gossiped about for some time, but one man claimed that he knew how much the man had left. He teased all the debaters and gossips in the village night after night. Eventually he let his big secret out, and the answer was that the rich man had left 'all of it' behind! No one in the village had been able to work out the mischievous man's little ruse because of the convergent thinking style they used.

Some exam questions may require you to be divergent in the way you think (that is, not just one obvious solution to the problem). This may mean being like a detective in the way you investigate and problem solve. The only difference is that you may need to set up the problem as well as the solution!

Get into the habit of 'stepping sideways' and looking at questions from several angles. The best way to do this is by practise, for example, on previous exam papers.

Checklist: Understanding questions fully

✓ Read over the chosen question several times.

✓ Write it down to ensure that it is clear.

✓ Check that you have not omitted any important aspect or point of emphasis.

✓ Ensure that you do not wrongly impose preconceived expectations on the question.

✓ Break the question into parts (dismantle and rebuild).

EXERCISE

Write your own checklist on any additional points of guidance for exams that you have picked up from tutors or textbooks.

....

....

....

....

....

When Asked to Discuss

Students often ask how much of their own opinion they should include in an essay. In a discussion, when you raise one issue, another one can arise out of it. One tutor used to introduce his lectures by saying that he was going to 'unpack' the arguments. When you unpack an object (such as a new desk that has to be assembled), you first remove the overall packaging, such as a large box, and then proceed to remove the covers from all the component parts. After that you attempt to assemble all the parts, according to the given design, so that they hold together in the intended manner. In a discussion your aim should be not just to identify and define all the parts that contribute, but also to show where they fit (or don't fit) into the overall picture.

> Although the word 'discuss' implies some allowance for your opinion, remember that this should be informed opinion rather than groundless speculation. There must also be direction, order, structure and end project.

Checklist: Features of a response to a 'discuss' question

- ✓ Contains a chain of issues that lead into each other in sequence.
- ✓ Clear shape and direction is unfolded in the progression of the argument.
- ✓ Underpinned by reference to findings and certainties.
- ✓ Identification of issues where doubt remains.
- ✓ Tone of argument may be tentative but should not be vague.

If a Critique is Requested

One example that might help clarify what is involved in a critique is the hotly debated topic of the physical punishment of children. It would be important in the interest of balance and fairness to present all sides and shades of the argument. You would then look at whether there is available evidence to support each argument, and you might introduce issues that have been coloured by prejudice, tradition, religion and legislation. It would be an aim to identify emotional arguments and arguments based on intuition and to get down to those arguments that really have solid evidence-based support. Finally, you would want to flag up where the strongest evidence appears to lie, and you should also identify issues that appear to be inconclusive. It would be expected that you should, if possible, arrive at some certainties.

EXERCISE

Write your own summary checklist for the features of a critique. You can either summarise the above points, or use your own points or a mixture of the two.

....

....

....

....

....

If Asked to Compare and Contrast

When asked to compare and contrast, you should be thinking in terms of similarities and differences. You should ask what the two issues share in common, and what features of each are distinct. Your preferred strategy for tackling this might be to work first through all the similarities, and then through all the contrasts (or vice versa). Alternatively, you could work through one similarity and contrast, followed by another similarity and contrast and so on.

Example: Write an essay that compares and contrasts theories of perception

1 *Similarities between theories*

(a) Explain perceptual phenomena, for example, depth cues, illusions and so on.
(b) Consideration of biological interaction.

2 Differences between theories

    (a) Focus on role of environment.

    (b) Focus on role of learning.

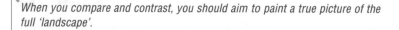

> *When you compare and contrast, you should aim to paint a true picture of the full 'landscape'.*

Whenever Evaluation is Requested

A worked example of evaluation is given below, based on a television soap opera director.

    Imagine that you are a television director for a popular soap opera. You have observed in recent months that you have lost some viewers to a soap opera on a rival channel. All is not yet lost because you still have a loyal hard core of viewers who have remained faithful. Your programme has been broadcast for ten years and there has, until recently, been little change in viewing figures. The rival programme has used some fresh ideas and new actors and has a big novelty appeal. It will take time to see if their level of viewing can be sustained, but you run the risk that you might lose some more viewers at least in the short term. On the other hand, with some imagination you might be able to attract some viewers back. However, there have been some recent murmurings about aspects of the programme being stale, repetitive and predictable. You have been given the task of evaluating the programme to see if you can ascertain why you have retained the faithful but lost other viewers, and what you could do to improve the programme without compromising the aspects that work. In your task you might want to review past features (retrospective), outline present features (perspective) and envisage positive future changes (prospective).

    This illustration may provoke you to think about how you might approach a question that asks you to evaluate some theory or concept in your own academic field of study. Some summary points to guide are presented below:

- Has the theory/concept stood the test of time?
- Is there a supportive evidence base that would not easily be overturned?
- Are there questionable elements that have been or should be challenged?
- Does more recent evidence point to a need for modification?

- Is the theory/concept robust and likely to be around for the foreseeable future?
- Could it be strengthened through being merged with other theories/concepts?

EXERCISE

Write your own checklist on what you remember or understand about each of the following: 'Discuss', 'Compare and Contrast', 'Evaluate' and 'Critique' (just a key word or two for each). If you find this difficult, then you should read the section again and then try the exercise.

....

....

....

....

It should be noted that the words presented in the above examples might not always be the exact words that will appear on your exam script – for example, you might find 'analyse' or 'outline' or 'investigate' and so on. The best advice is to check over past exam papers and familiarise yourself with the words that are most recurrent.

3.8	
summary	

Part Three has been designed to give you reference points to measure where you are at in your studies, and to help you map out the way ahead in manageable increments. It should now be clear that learning should not merely be a mechanical exercise, such as just memorising and reproducing study material. Quality learning also involves making connections between ideas, thinking at a deeper level by attempting to understand your material, and developing a critical approach to learning. However, this cannot be achieved without the discipline of preparation for lectures, seminars and exams, or without learning to structure your material (headings and subheadings) and to set each unit of learning within its overall context in your subject and programme. An important device in learning is to develop the ability to ask questions (whether written, spoken or silent). Another useful device in learning is to illustrate your material and use examples that will help make your study fun, memorable and vivid. It is useful to set problems for yourself that will allow you to think through solutions and therefore enhance the quality of your learning.

On the one hand, there are the necessary disciplined procedures such as preparation before each learning activity and consolidation afterwards. It is also vital to keep your subject materials in organised folders so that you can add/extract/replace materials when you need to. On the other hand, there is the need to develop personality qualities such as feeding your confidence, fuelling your motivation and turning stress responses to your advantage. Part Three has presented strategies to guide you through finding the balance between these organised and dynamic aspects of academic life.

Your aim should be to become an 'all-round student' who engages in and benefits from all the learning activities available to you (lectures, seminars, tutorials, computing, labs, discussions, library work and so on), and to develop all the academic and personal skills that will put you in the driving seat to academic achievement. It will be motivating and confidence building for you, if you can recognise the value of these qualities, both across your academic programme and beyond graduation to the world of work. They will also serve you well in your continued commitment to lifelong learning.

glossary

Abstract rule theory (Braine & O'Brien, 1991)

Reason is determined by mental logic and abstract, content-free rules are used. Mistakes are made because the original problem either is misunderstood or is difficult and exceeds working memory capability. Direct reasoning involves the use of schemas, which help form conclusions, but indirect reasoning has to rely on other systems (such as domain-specific ones), which may lead to response bias. Errors can be made in terms of comprehending or representing the problem, actioning the appropriate schemas or inadequate and incorrect processing.

Accommodation

Depth perception results from the thickening of the lens when looking at close objects.

Aerial perspective

Distant objects lose contrast because light is dispersed as it travels through the atmosphere.

Affirmation of the consequence

A common mistake made in reasoning where people assume that because B is true (I have bought clothes), then A must be true (there was a sale); however, since there are a number of reasons why people buy clothes, it is not valid to claim there was a sale.

Aggrammatism	Insufficient grammatical structure in production. Even though people have a knowledge of appropriate words or grammar, they lack the right words to say and may even resort to using made up words.
Algorithmic methods	Based on principles that encourage a systematic search through every possible solution. Although this offers a guaranteed solution, the problem lies in the fact that it is very time consuming.
Anomia	People are unable to name objects.
Anticipated regret	If we believe we will regret a decision, then we are likely to avoid that decision even though it might have been a good one to make. Therefore, actions may be avoided to prevent such regret (*omission bias* – Baron, 1997).
Anticipation and perseverated errors – Dell et al. (1997)	Specifically outlined anticipatory and perseverated errors as those most common in language production (words being spoken either before or after they should have been). As such, anticipatory errors are most common in experts who are planning delivery of speech and perseverated errors are less common because of prior experience/practise.
Aphasia	Language is understood but cannot be produced (jargon aphasia) or there are difficulties in understanding language (fluent aphasia).
Apparent motion	Motion can be perceived even in the absence of movement, so a light that is flashing on and off is seen as moving because such movements are seen as one rather than two separate parts.

Attentional engagement theory (Duncan & Humphreys, 1989, 1992)

All items are analysed in terms of their features and then a later stage of processing occurs where input is matched for its likeness in STM. Here, speed is determined by the amount of desegregation required and the similarity present in non-target items; thus items that are similar will be selected together.

Attenuation theory (Treisman, 1960)

Assumes that the non-attended input is not rejected but is 'attenuated' (diminished) compared to attended information. All attenuated channels are then analysed semantically (that is, information is selected for its meaning) and information that has either personal important or current relevance is recognised thus making an output response possible.

Automatic processing

Occurs when tasks are practised and therefore require less attention, so it is easier to perform them simultaneously. Eysenck & Keane (2000: p. 141) state that automatic processes are ones that are fast, demand little attention/don't reduce capacity for performance, are unavailable to consciousness and are unavoidable.

Availability heuristic

As familiar/recent events are more readily available to memory then they are seen as more probable; therefore, estimates of probability are dependent on past recollections and retrieval of information from LTM. Thus, it is based partly on occurrence, with a correlation between frequency and subsequent judgement on the basis of the perceived probability.

Bayes' theorem (Eysenck & Keane, 2000: p. 476)

To make any judgement we need to take into account the probability of the two beliefs/hypotheses in a given situation before new data was obtained (*prior odds*) and the relative probability of obtaining the data under each hypothesis (*posterior odds*).

Binocular cues

Require the use of both eyes in perception.

Bottleneck theories

A bottleneck makes it harder for two descriptions to be made similar. This is supported by the psychological refractory period, which is the delay caused by the increased information processing time when a second stimulus closely follows the first.

Bottom-up theory of perception – (Gibson, 1950, 1966, 1979)

Perception results from sensation initially derived from the optic array, which picks up consistent information from the environment and does so even when there is interaction with different aspects of the environment (the consistency being referred to as invariants). Since this means that light is reaching the eye, it allows perception of depth, location and so on. Resonance aids the process whereby environmental stimuli are picked up and tuned into as an automatic process. Information thus takes the form of optic flow patterns (giving information on speed and direction of movement), texture gradients (closer objects seen in more detail than further ones) and affordances (detail about the function of objects).

Bridging inferences

Link current and preceding text with elaborative inferences that enhance understanding with detail.

Capacity

How much information is stored in memory. This varies with the memory store, for example, seven, plus or minus two items in STM and an unlimited amount in LTM.

Capacity theory (Just & Carpenter, 1992)

Focuses on working memory (or the central executive that deals with language comprehension in the WMM). Working memory stores and processes language in a limited capacity during processing; therefore the main assumption is that when people are assessed using reading span tasks there are individual differences in their language comprehension because there are individual differences in their working memory capacity. MRI work also shows that the same areas of the brain are involved in reading span as in sentence comprehension and that there is more activity in Wernicke's area when asked to read and maintain information rather than reading it alone.

Case studies

These focus on one individual and their behaviour, thoughts, feelings and experiences.

Central capacity theory (Kahneman, 1973)

This model is seen as being more flexible, with one central processor responsible for allocating attention. Attention is therefore a skill more than a simple process. Capacity is limited but varies. Most attention will be devoted to tasks where there is a high level of difficulty. The capacity available is dependent upon arousal level and attention is allocated according to the effort required, current goals/objectives and importance.

Central executive

This is a control system and is most important because it is responsible for monitoring and coordinating the 'slave systems'. It is flexible as it can process visual and auditory information (so is modality free) and has some limited storage capacity.

Chunking

According to Miller (1956), separate pieces of information can be combined to form a chunk.

Cognitive neuropsychology

Looks at brain functioning using biological techniques to understand human cognitions. For example, single-unit recording looks at the working of single neurons and is a sensitive technique that examines electrical changes; an EEG uses electrodes attached to the scalp to detect small changes in electrical activity in the brain, while a PET scan can detect positrons emitted from radioactive water injected into the human body; and MRI measures radio waves that when excited by atoms produce magnetic changes detected by magnets – a computer then interprets these changes and produces 3-D images.

Cognitive neuroscience

Looks at impaired cognitive processes (for example, brain damage) in order to understand normal cognitions. It uses dissociations and is useful because it allows us to see the processes and mechanics involved in normal cognitive functioning. There is, however, a problem with using single dissociations, as a good performance on one task rather than another may simply be due to confounding variables, such as task complexity, and it is therefore better to look at double dissociations, that is, compare impaired performance on tasks between different patients. Theoretical assumptions of this model include the following: the idea that cognitive systems are modular; the brain and mind are related with specific functions in specific areas of the brain; and impaired cognitive functioning can tell us much about normal cognitive functioning.

Cohort theory (Marslen-Wilson & Tyler, 1980)

A word initial cohort is derived from sounds which then activate recognised words that have been presented auditorally. If they do not match the presented information or relate to the context or meaning of the word, then they are eliminated and the recognition point simply occurs when this matching processing is complete and all other possibilities have indeed been eliminated. Thus there is an interaction and combination of all language aspects such as meaning, grammar, etc. before word recognition takes place.

Computational theory (Marr, 1982)

Individuals construct and then work through three hierarchical stages of representation before being able to recognise an object. An initial (retinal) representation (described by Marr as having two phases: 'the raw primal sketch', which recognises various light intensities; and 'the full primal sketch' which outlines shapes) provides basic information about the features of the object to form a 2.5-D sketch. At the second stage of representation, individuals interpret the 2.5-D sketch from their own particular point of view. Finally at the third stage, binocular disparity enables individuals to process more detailed information about the object, for example, depth (using the range map) and orientation, and subsequently construct a 3-D model based on the simple construction of an image (accessibility), its scope and uniqueness, and the similarities shared by and differences between objects (stability and sensitivity) (Marr & Nishihara, 1978).

Cognitive science

Uses computational/computer models to understand cognitions. It allows specification of a theory to predict behaviour. Flowcharts are used to construct theories and provide a plan from which input can be examined as well as the nature of storage and decision processes. This information can then be used to devise a computer program. There are three main types of computational modelling techniques: semantic networks, production changes and connectionist networks.

**Connectionist approach
(Plaut et al., 1996)**

Proposed that the pronunciation of all words relies on interactive, rather than separate, mechanisms. Specifically, connections exist between visual form and combinations of letters and their basic sound (phonemes). The model predicted, and research showed, that naming was more difficult/took longer for inconsistent and rare words, whilst there were few difficulties in pronouncing consistent words, because the match was greater between the visual forms and phonemes. Research into surface and phonological dyslexia has provided further support for this model.

**Connectionist model
(Farah & McClelland, 1991)**

A number of systems are connected in this computational model: visual and verbal systems linked by a semantic system. Thus a visual representation is made and the name of the object is coded within the verbal system. Object recognition proceeds through a series of stages, from the visual, to the semantic and then the verbal system. Here, the semantic system is key, since it links visual characteristics to functions of objects. Thus all aspects are connected – hence the model's title).

Connectionist networks

Use modelling techniques that suggest networks have structures and layers which are connected together (like neurons/nodes). Concepts are stored within the network and are activated by patterns, which are simply the associations between inputs and outputs, and especially important is back-propogation, which uses a comparison of actual and correct responses.

**Constraint-based theory
(MacDonald et al., 1994)**

Parallel processes operate and are constrained by semantic and grammatical knowledge, and analyses of these is therefore simultaneous. When a sentence is ambiguous four assumptions are made/used: grammatical knowledge of possible intent, association of words are not independent, ambiguity, and past experience determines interpretations made.

Construction integration model – (Kintsch, 1988, 1992, 1994)

Propositions derive from sentences and enter a short-term buffer (propositional net). Inferences are then added from LTM leading to an elaborated propositional net (inclusive of irrelevant details). An integration process then occurs where connected structures are selected to form text representations stored in episodic text memory. So, if two pieces of information were processed together in the original short-term buffer store, then the relationship between them will have been retained throughout the process. Therefore discourse processing/language comprehension uses three levels of representation: surface representation (actual text), propositional representation (text-based propositions) and situational representations (a mind map/ mental model based on schemas constructed from the situational representations in the text).

Controlled processing

Is slow, makes heavy demands and has a limited capacity, but encourages flexible processing and requires direct attention.

Convergence

Depth is perceived because when an object is close the eyes turn inwards to focus on it.

Co-operative principle (Grice, 1967)

Predicts that speakers and listeners must co-operate when producing language and ideally, cues such as rhythm, stress and intonation (prosodic cues) are used.

Correlation

Measures the strength of the relationship between two variables; for example, it tests if there is a relationship between two things. It does not, however, test cause and effect – so it does not say that one thing causes the other, but simply says there is some relationship between two things.

Cue dependent forgetting

Information cannot be accessed so it is available but not accessible and can't be rehearsed.

Cyclic theory (Neisser, 1976)

Perception involves both bottom-up and top-down elements. It is simply the result of a cyclic (circular) process where previous learning/schemas inform the information processing of perceptual stimuli, but when environmental stimuli fail to match such knowledge, then the schema has to be adapted so it is a constant process of adaptation.

Decision making

Involves making significant and personal choices when provided with options, in other words, making a cost–benefit analysis.

Deductive reasoning

Where a logical conclusion is made following a statement that is usually true. It is based on what is called the 'propositional calculus', which involves logical operators, for example, not, and, or, if … then, if and only if. Such logic put more simply involves making decisions where 'if A happens then conclusion B can be drawn'. Truth tables are used to work out if a statement is true or false so that reasoning can take place and to provide a guide on what inferences are correct or incorrect according to logic.

Denial of the antecedent

Here, A is false (there is *no* sale) and people commonly assume that this means B (I have *not* bought clothes) is false as well. However, as stated above, the absence of a sale does not preclude people from buying clothes, which means again that no firm conclusion can be made.

Dependent variable (DV)

This is what one hopes alters as a result of what is *changed* (so the DV measures any changes the IV has produced).

Differentiation theory of perceptual development

Perception develops once distinctive features of objects can be transferred across situations and once they can be differentiated from irrelevant stimuli. Such differentiation tends to occur as a product of age.

Discourse processing (Kintsch & Van Dijk, 1978)

To comprehend language, analyses are made both of the argument (semantic representation) and of the position (giving meaning to the smallest component of a story, for example, a phrase within it). These meanings are given as a result of processing within a limited capacity STM store and bridging inferences amongst other things. Therefore, important propositions most relevant to understanding the story have subsequently better recall because they spend longer in this buffer. Irrelevant propositions are deleted, generalised or single propositions constructed from numerous ones. Discourse occurs at two processing levels: micro (where the smallest components are connected) and macro (where the story is formed by editing the smaller details to give an overall picture.

Displacement

Forgetting occurs in the STM because old items have been displaced (replaced) by new pieces of information and therefore the original items are lost.

Divided attention

Looks at how attention can be devoted to more than one input stimulus and what the capacities are on this.

Domain-specific theories

Initially, an overall mechanism controls reasoning, but it then becomes a more specific process because a second mechanism acknowledges the importance of domain-specific schemas. In other words, previous knowledge and experience aids reasoning of different situations. Pragmatic reasoning schemata are used to reason conclusions about everyday situations. Although these can potentially apply to a wide range of situations, in practice they are limited by goals and general relationships between things. For example, obligation schemata aid reasoning of a situation where you feel obliged to do something. Social contract theory (Cosmides, 1989) believes that domain-specific rules exist in accordance within the Darwinian theory of evolution and that reasoning rests on the idea that ensures goal achievement in the social context to enhance survival.

**Dual-route model
(Ellis & Young, 1988)**

The visual system has to initially identify and group sets of letters presented textually, and the process of converting text to sound then involves three routes. Firstly, the grapheme– phoneme conversion occurs where the written word is converted to sound using punctuation and applying typical rules to translate (groups of) letters. Thus pronunciation of regular spelling-sound words and non-words is possible. Route two involves the lexicon and semantic systems (dictionary and meaning systems). Here, a word is perceived and then a search for its representation is sought in the visual input lexicon, following which, its meaning is identified from the semantic system and the word is spoken. Support for the function of this route can be obtained from phonological and deep dyslexics. Lastly, a lexicon-only route can be employed resembling the processes identified above but meaning is not considered; therefore visual input and speech output lexicons are used to produce familiar and regular (rule-based) words (but not unfamiliar and non-words).

Duration

Refers to how long a piece of information is retained in memory. This is believed to be approximately 15–30 seconds in STM and for an unlimited time in LTM.

Encoding

Refers to how information is coded into the memory system. In SM it is believed to be both acoustic (according to sound) and visual (according to sight), whilst in STM it is mainly visual and then in LTM it is semantic/coded according to its meaning.

Encoding specificity principle

The overlap between information at recall/recognition and that in the original memory trace, will determine retrieval.

Enrichment theory

Infants usually develop their sensory and motor abilities in the sensori-motor stage before the age of two and their subsequent interaction with the world aids the development of innate schemas. After this, they are able to form new schemas through the process of accommodation. Perception therefore occurs because it is influenced by the expectations that result from such schemas.

Episodic memory

Involves the storage and retrieval of specific events (including place and time).

Event indexing model (Zwaan & Radvansky, 1990)

To understand stories/comprehend language several aspects are analysed: the protagonist, the relationship between current and past events, the relationship between such events and their spatial relationship and the relationship between goals and previous events. In other words, temporality, causality, spatiality and intentionality. It is difficult to comprehend or construct an idea of the situation if these aspects do not match up.

Experimental cognitive psychology

Places an experimental emphasis on cognitive psychology.

**E–Z reader model
(Reichle et al., 1998)**

Readers assess the familiarity of a word whilst looking at it and this triggers eye movement and lexical access/decisions about the meaning of a word, after which attention progresses to the following word. Unsurprisingly, lexical and frequency decisions are faster for more common and predictable words. In other words, reading occurs on a word-by-word basis.

Face recognition

Focuses on the processes involved in recognising faces.

**Face recognition
(Bruce & Young, 1986)**

Eight components are involved in recognising faces: an initial description (structural encoding), analysis of expression, analysis of facial speech, selective processing of facial information (directed visual processing), constructing information about faces, identifying nodes about personal information, storing the person's name, and adding any other important information. As such, recognition of familiar and unfamiliar faces can take place. Eysenck & Keane (2000) suggest that recognition of familiar faces principally involves structural encoding, face recognition, personal information and naming, whilst recognition of unfamiliar faces involves encoding, expression and facial speech analysis, and direct visual processing.

Familiar size

Previous experience about object size can be used to judge distance.

**Feature integration theory
(Treisman, 1988/1992)**

There is a distinction between objects and their features (for example, colour) where all basic features are processed rapidly, in parallel and in an automatic, pre-attentive way. Features are combined in a serial process – to form objects – which is influenced by knowledge, but in the absence of knowledge, illusions may be created.

Feature theory

Focuses on the idea that there are key features within patterns which are perceived and compared to information already held in memory. There is some discussion as to whether a detailed analysis leads to a general assumption, or vice versa. Visual search research supports these ideas, for example, identifying the target letter Z took less time if it was set amongst rounded rather than straight letters, because the rounded letters shared fewer common features so could be compared more rapidly (Neisser, 1964).

Filter theory (Broadbent, 1958)

Two similar stimuli gain parallel access to a sensory register that briefly holds the information; a selective filter then allows one input through on the basis of physical characteristics and the other channel rests in the buffer. This is followed by some limited capacity processing and an output response. The importance of the filter, therefore, is that it prevents overload.

Focused/selective attention

Concentrates on how attention is focused on a particular input stimulus, why it is selective and what happens to the non-attended stimuli.

Forgetting

When information is temporarily or permanently unavailable. This may be because it has been replaced by new information, has faded from memory, has suffered from interference or lack of available cues or is forgotten due to emotional factors/anxiety. Forgetting can therefore occur within short- and long-term memory systems.

Framing

Presents particular problems when testing decision making, because it is concerned with the phrasing or presentation of a problem.

Garden path model (Frazier & Rayner, 1982)

One element of a sentence is considered (the simplest one) because this involves minimal attachment (for example, has the fewest sentence parts) and then late closure occurs (where new words are attached to the phrase). Therefore, meaning or prior content does not affect selection.

Guided search theory (Wolfe, 1998)

Similar to feature integration theory as there is an initial feature based, then subsequent general search process. It is not, however, assumed that processing is parallel then serial. Instead, initial feature processing produces an activation map, with each input showing individual levels; attention is then allocated on the basis of highest–lowest activation.

Heuristic and bias accounts

Most people are inherently logical but biases/heuristics override this.

Implicit learning

'Learning complex information without complete verbalisable knowledge of what is learned' (Seger, 1994 in Eysenck & Keane, 2000, p. 63).

Independent variable (IV)

This is the thing that the researcher *deliberately manipulates* and so it is the thing that she purposely changes.

Inductive reasoning

General conclusions drawn about particular statements, often based on previous experience. For example, 'Every time I have kicked a ball in the air it has come back down.' So if I kick a ball up in the air again, inductive reasoning would suggest that it is logical to predict that it will come back down again.

Inferences

'The core of the understanding process', (Schank, 1976 in Eysenck & Keane, 2000 p. 168).

Information criterion

The assumption that information provided by the participant must be responsible for improved performance.

Interactive activation and competition model (Humphreys et al. 1995)

Structural descriptions of visually similar objects generate semantic and then name representations and each of these are connected.

Interactive activation model – (McClelland & Rumelhart, 1981)

Three levels are involved in word recognition: the feature level, letter level (identifying letter positioning within a word) and the recognising of the actual word. Bottom-up processing therefore operates from feature to word via letter whilst the opposite is true for top-down processing. It works such that any words containing similar features or letters are activated whilst all other possibilities are inhibited, so that one word is left to be recognised. Later developments of the model tried to account for the speed as well as accuracy of recognition.

Interposition

An object that is near hinders perception of another object because it essentially hides the other object from view.

Judgements

These involve looking at the conclusions we draw on the basis of available evidence and knowledge, and is usually concerned with statistical judgements.

Late selection theory (Deutsch & Deutsch, 1963)

Assumes that all input is analysed equally for meaning and the filter occurs as a result of a late selection process. Selection will again be based on relevance of the input.

Law of closure

Missing parts are filled in to allow perception of the whole.

Law of good continuation

Elements that are mostly uninterrupted are seen as continuous.

Law of Pragnanz

Perceptual organisation 'will always be as "good" as the prevailing conditions allow' (Koffka, 1935, p. 110).

Law of proximity
Parts of an object that are close to each other will be grouped together and perceived as a whole.

Law of similarity
Patterns that are visually similar are grouped together. The method then involves evaluating the probability of observing the data if hypothesis A and B are correct. Thus judgements are made on the basis of the probability of outcomes subsequent to new evidence.

Letter identification
It was originally assumed that individual letters require recognition as a prerequisite to recognising words; however, contradictory thought suggests that words have superiority over letters and actually aid letter recognition rather than vice versa.

Linear perspective
Parallel lines pointing away are perceived to be closer together when viewed in the distance.

Long-term memory (LTM)
According to Atkinson and Shiffrin's (1968) multistore model of memory, the LTM is a memory store that processes information according to its meaning (semantically) and which holds an unlimited amount for a lengthy period of time. Information for LTM flows from the STM.

Loss aversion
When making decisions we tend to focus more on what we could lose rather than what we could gain.

Means-ends analysis
One of the most important heuristic methods and involves recognising the difference between current and goal states, creating a subgoal to reduce this and then selecting an operator to solve the subgoal (Eysenck & Flanagan, 2000).

Mental models

These are constructed on the basis of possibilities and a conclusion is reached when these are verified. No other examples can be sought. Again, if a large number of models have to be considered before a conclusion is drawn, then working memory capability may be exceeded, thus leading to mistakes being made. These tend to arise specifically when different interpretations are made of an assumption and therefore fail to draw upon the most helpful mental model in their reasoning process.

Minimalist hypothesis (McKoon & Ratcliff, 1992)

States that inferences are automatic (where general knowledge is used to combine sentences coherently, or where information is explicit in the text or where they are directed and are therefore formed to achieve a goal). This is different to constructionist hypotheses, as it is predicted that there are constraints on the number of automatic inferences that are made.

Missionaries and cannibals problem – (Simon & Reed, 1976)

Believed three specific heuristics could be used to solve this problem. People were asked how three missionaries and three cannibals can cross a river when the boat holds a maximum of two and where more cannibals than missionaries cannot be left on the bank otherwise the missionaries will be eaten. The heuristics were: *balance strategies* (equal numbers of each remain), *means-ends strategy* (used in an attempt to reach the subgoal); and *anti-looping strategies* (which avoid backtracking on moves already made towards solutions). The most critical move is the transition made from balance to means–ends.

Modular theory (Allport, 1989)

Proposes that attention consists of several specific information processing modules for information, each with its own resources and capacities. Similar tasks interfere if they therefore use the same module's resources, but in parallel processing it can occur if they are dissimilar, as interference is not created.

Modus ponens

If A is true (there is a sale in the shop), then B is also true (I will buy clothes).

Modus tollens

If B is false (that is, I have **not** bought clothes), then A is also false (that is, there was **no** sale in the shop).

Monocular cues

Require the use of one eye.

Motion parallax

images that are nearer appear to be going faster than those that are further away.

Motor theory – (Liberman, Cooper, Shankweiler & Studdet-Kennedy, 1967)

Listeners copy the speech/motor movements made by the speaker and so can recognise words even when the context may be ambiguous.

Multistore model (MSM) of memory

A model of memory proposed by Atkinson and Shiffrin (1968) which assumes that there are three separate memory stores (SM, STM and LTM), that information must flow from one store to the next, and that it can only be retained in STM if rehearsal has taken place.

Object recognition

Recognising objects, including from different orientations and distances.

Observations

Look at the behaviour of participants in various situations and see 'a relatively unconstrained segment of a person's freely chosen behaviour as it occurs' (Coolican, 1990). These can be structured or unstructured, but can be carried out in the participant's natural environment.

Oculomotor cues	Are those that use the muscles around both eyes.
Operationalise	Definition of a concept.
Opponent process theory	Processing occurs because colour receptors are organised into two pairs – red–green and blue–yellow. When one is activated it prevents activation of the other.
Pandemonium model of feature detection (Selfridge, 1959)	Four hierarchical stages are involved in processing features and this process occurs in parallel using an analogy of demons. Initially, an object is represented as an image, which is a biological process where it falls onto the retina (image demon), and features are then analysed and compared, for instance, for lines and angles (the feature demon). Subsequently, components are recognised and meaningful patterns constructed (cognitive demons) and lastly, patterns are recognised as a result of this matching process.
Parsing	Analysis of syntax, or grammatical structure's 'set of rules'. Grammatical structure can be ambiguous in terms of comprehension either at a *global* level (the sentence has more than one interpretation) or at the *local* level (varying interpretations could be made at different stages of processing).
Pattern recognition	The categorisation of 2-D patterns.
Pendulum problem (Maier, 1931)	People were brought into a room where there were two lengths of strings hanging from the ceiling and a number of objects lying about, for example, poles, pliers, extension cables. Their task was to tie the strings together; however, the strings were too far apart to reach each other. The pendulum problem can be insightfully solved by tying

pliers to the ends of the strings and swinging both to catch them in the middle.

Perceived justification

Decisions are made on the basis to which they can be justified. Tversky & Shafir (1992) found that of three exam groups who could go to Hawaii for a cheap holiday, those who knew they had either passed or failed could justify going because they felt they were justified in either celebrating or recovering. On the other hand, the group whose results were unknown could not justify it to themselves and were more likely to stay and await their grade.

Perception

According to Hill (2001), perception involves detecting a feature or object, perceiving depth and recognising patterns or objects.

Phonemic restoration effect

Using context to fill in (hence restore) parts of a missing sentence. Occurs because of sensitivity and response bias effects.

Phonological loop

Has an articulatory control system (verbal rehearsal, time-based, inner voice) and a phonological store (speech-based storage system, inner ear). It holds information for a short period of time – so stores a limited number of sounds for brief seconds (an 'inner ear'). It has two components: the phonological store, which stores sound for a brief period of time; and the articulatory control system, which allows repetition of stored items/is a verbal rehearsal system.

Phonological theory of reading – (Frost, 1998)

Emphasised the role of phonological coding (sound) and believed it to be an automatic and fundamental part of reading or process-ing text, occurring rapidly when a word is presented visually. As such, he predicted that it occurs even if it does not help (or in fact actually impairs) reading.

Pragmatics

Analysis of semantics, or how language is used to communicate a message. It is argued that a sentence has three different types of force/meaning – locutionary force (literal meaning), illocutionary force (goal/ intended meaning) and perlocutionary force (actual effect) – which must all be used in order to comprehend language.

Primacy-recency effect

Items at the start or end of a list are recalled better than those in the middle, because those at the start can still be accessed from STM and those at the end have been rehearsed and can be accessed from LTM.

Proactive interference

Old material prevents new information from being remembered; forgetting occurs because of the interference of the old material.

Probabilistic theory (Oaksford & Chater, 1994, 1995, 1996)

Reasoning is simply based on the probability of gaining information whilst reducing uncertainty.

Problem-space theory (Newell & Simon, 1972)

Problems have a structure that can be viewed as a set of states (initial-goal state). Operations are applied (actions taken) that move one through these problem-solving states, sometimes leading to dead ends, other times to discovery such that movement occurs towards the goal. People use their knowledge and heuristics to do this, so a person's prior knowledge is crucial to their problem-solving.

Production changes

Are made up of rules ('if ... then ...') that are held in the LTM of a production system that also contains a working memory where information that is being processed is held. The system operates by matching such processed information with the 'if' part of the rule to produce the appropriate ('then') response. Strategies are also used to select the most appropriate response.

Protoype theory

Proposes that there is a matching process which is very specific since only one prototype exists for a given category; thus a comparison takes place such that the pattern is either recognised or not, and if not it is then subsequently compared to another prototype.

Questionnaires

Use fixed and/or open-ended questions to make a quick and efficient assessment of people's attitudes.

Recall

Involves searching memory with few external cues.

Recognition

Involves matching material to external information.

Recognition-by-components theory – (Biederman, 1987)

Developed from Marr's work, this approach suggests that 36 basic shapes are recognised (geons) and pattern recognition occurs once the combination and spatial arrangement of these are identified. Identification of five 'invariant properties' are required, that is, more simply, if the edges are straight, converging, parallel, symmetrical or curving, these are then matched to the images/templates already held in memory. As part of this process, it means recognition can take place even if only part of the object can be viewed and when some information is not retrievable.

Reconstructive memory

When information is recalled it tends to be distorted because we change it to fit into existing schemas of information (building blocks of knowledge) that we hold; therefore expectations lead us to reconstruct memories.

Reconstructive memory (Bartlett, 1932)	Believed that schemas (the building blocks of knowledge derived from previous experience) were fundamental for language comprehension. Based on his storytelling of an Indian folk tale, 'War of the Ghosts', he found that we do not in fact recall information accurately but instead reconstruct language based on such expectations ('effort after meaning'). Accounts of the story were distorted in several ways by westerners, for example, omissions were made, there were changes of order, rationalisation, alterations in importance and distortions of emotion.
Representativeness heuristic	'Estimating the probability of a particular sample of events based on their similarity to characteristics we feel are typical of the whole category population of those events' (Hill, 2001, p. 137)
Repression	According to Freud, when memories are associated with an unpleasant feeling they are forgotten and pushed into the unconscious to avoid distress.
Retrieval	How information can be retrieved from memory and whether it is unavailable or simply inaccessible.
Retrieval failure	Forgetting occurs because the correct cues are unavailable, so information is forgotten because the cues used to code it are no longer available in LTM.
Retroactive interference	New material prevents old information from being remembered; thus forgetting occurs because of the interference of the new material.
Rule application hypothesis (Hayes & Simon, 1977)	The easier the rules are to apply to the problem, then the more quickly and easily it will be solved.

Rule learning hypothesis (Kotovsky et al., 1985)	Problems will be solved more easily when the rules for solving them are clearer and quick to pick up.
Schema	A building block of knowledge derived from previous experience and subsequent expectations and they are formed from early childhood.
Scientific method	Means that you need to test a hypothesis to examine variables that influence behaviour. Thus the hypothesis states that two variables are related in some way and altering one of them may cause the participant to alter the other.
Script-pointer-plus tag hypothesis – (Schank & Abelson, 1977)	Developed Bartlett's ideas in that they still focused on schemas and scripts, but Eysenck and Keane (2000) state that they redeveloped some of the ideas to suggest that there is a combining of material from the story and schema and note is made of typical or untypical actions within the story (that is, whether or not they are consistent with these underlying scripts). Recognition memory and recall is then better for atypical actions because they are easier to discriminate and thus are tagged individually in memory. However, over time typical actions are better recalled because of their link to well-established schemas.
Search-after-meaning theory – (Graesser et al., 1994)	Readers use their goals to give meaning to text and then use these to explain and comprehend actions/events in the text. Specifically, it involves giving meaning to the text based on goals (reader goal assumption); this has to be coherent (coherence assumption) and is used to explain events (explanation assumption).

Semantic memory	Stores information/meaning about the world including general and abstract facts.
Semantic networks	Where concepts are linked by a network of nodes that represent general (associative/ similar) relationships, specific relationships or complete ones. The strength of these links will vary according to the similarity of different concepts, and learning occurs when new links are added or the strength of the relationship changes.
Semantic priming effect	When sentences contain words that add meaning or context, then recognition is faster, probably because such priming leads to the activation of related words stored within memory and because this occurs after lexical processing.
Sensitivity criterion	Must acknowledge that participants may know more than they are being tested on so underestimate their knowledge as a result.
Sensory Memory (SM)	The initial memory store into which all visual and acoustic information form the environment enters the memory system to be further processed or discarded.
Shading	Helps depth perception, as it only occurs with 3-D objects.
Short-term memory (STM)	According to Atkinson and Shiffrin's multistore model of memory, the STM is a memory store that processes information visually (according to sight) and acoustically (according to sound) and which holds a limited amount (seven, plus or minus two items) for a short period of time (15–30 seconds) unless rehearsal occurs. Information for STM flows from the SM and then into the LTM.

Spotlight theory	Resembles the idea that we have a small field of vision and it is hard to see things outside of this spotlight region, although attention can be shifted by moving this light.
Spreading activation theory – (Dell, 1986; Dell & O'Seaghdha, 1991)	The theory predicts that several common errors will be made in speech production. Principally, they are anticipatory errors (where words are spoken 'in anticipation' too early in the sentence and exchange errors (where words are 'exchanged' or swapped around), although multiple errors are possible. The lexical bias effect suggests that errors in language production are made using either actual words or basic word forms. This is because speech production involves more advanced processing at the highest of the four levels of processing, that is, at the semantic/meaning level not at the syntactic/grammatical level, morphological/basic word forms and phonological level, and errors occur because incorrect items are sometimes activated more readily than correct ones.
Stereopsis	Refers to the way in which depth is perceived when images are projected onto the retina of both eyes.
Storage	How information in memory is stored.
Story grammar	A set of rules from which the structure of the story is derived, usually in a hierarchy of importance, for example, plot before characters.
Story processing	In order to comprehend a story, evidence has shown that we interpret some aspects and leave out others – mainly focusing on important events.
Sunk-cost effect	Additional resources are used to further support a previous commitment (as in the saying 'throwing good money after bad').

Synthesis theory (Baddeley, 1986)

Based on the idea of the working memory model – modality free, central, limited capacity processing and therefore modality processing systems.

Tachistoscope

A machine that allows very rapid presentation of stimulus material.

Template theory

Argues that LTM contains templates of patterns which are matched to the visual input and involves various templates.

Texture

Objects that slant away have a texture gradient that increases as you look at them from front to back.

Top-down theory of processing – (Gregory 1972)

Predicts that perception is an active process that is based on experience and expectations. Thus schemas (past knowledge, expectations and so on) make inferences about perceptual data. Perceptual constancies and illusions support this notion, that is, the size, shape and location of objects remain the same even when they are seen from different distances, angles and locations because the brain uses schemas to compensate for these changes and interprets on the basis of experience and expectations. A similar process occurs with illusions, of which there are numerous. To give just some examples, this process applies to distortions, ambiguous figures, paradoxical figures and fictions. Perceptual set is therefore also important. This is where previous experience, expectations, motivation and emotion create a bias towards the perception of particular stimuli (or aspects of them) whilst ignoring other available data.

Tower of Hanoi (Newell & Simon, 1972)

When shown three vertical pegs in a row, people were asked to reallocate three-size ordered discs from the first to the last peg (initial-goal state). However, there are a number of set rules when solving this problem: only one disc can be moved at a time and a larger disc cannot go on top of a smaller one.

Trace Decay

A theory of forgetting in STM because it states that over time memory traces simply fade away.

TRACE model (McClelland & Elman, 1986)/McClelland, 1991)

There is an interaction of many features of language but most importantly that data-driven processes resulting from things we hear (bottom-up processing) interact with the concepts taken from linguistic context (top-down processing). Units containing the features of speech, the sounds and words are connected progressively (so features to sounds, sounds to words in bottom-up processing and vice versa for top-down processing). The interaction between these levels is, however, dependent on their activation, where a trace is formed based on the spreading of information between such units, whilst subject to excitation and inhibitory processes.

Trichromatic theory

Three types of cone receptor account for colour perception, that is, receptors for blue, green and red. These are derived from the fact that each cone receptor has varying sensitivity: the first, to short-wavelength light; the second, to medium-; and the last, to long-wave-length, respectively, responding to each of the aforementioned colours. When combined, however, they can produce perception of any other colour.

Two-process theory

States that whilst recall involves a retrieval process followed by a recognition process based on the matching of the retrieved information, recognition only involves the matching of material to external information. Therefore, as recall involves two stages recognition only one, then recognition is better.

Utility theory – (Neumann & Morgenstern, 1947)

When making decisions we try to assess the value of an outcome or 'maximise utility'. To do this we weigh up the probability of a given outcome and the utility (value) of the outcome. Hence: [Expected utility = (probability of a given outcome) x (utility of the outcome)]

Visual cliff experiment

A table top was designed whereby a check pattern was placed under one side (shallow end) and on the floor beneath the top on the other (deep end). Results found that babies (6½ –12 months old) were reluctant to crawl onto the deep side.

Visual preference task

Young infants (4 days–5 months old) were shown discs that either were blank or features that resembled those of the human face in the correct position or jumbled up and showed a preference for the discs that most closely resembled the face.

Visuo-spatial scratch pad

('Inner eye'). – is designed for temporary storage and manipulation of spatial and visual information. It has a limited capacity but limits for visual and spatial systems are different (so you can rehearse a set of digits whilst also making spatial decisions). According to Logie (1995) it can be subdivided into the visual cache, which stores information about visual form and colour, and the inner scribe, which holds spatial and movement information.

Water jug problem (Luchins & Luchins, 1959)

There were two groups. One was given problems that could be solved using the same solution repeatedly and the other, problems that required different solutions. A subsequent problem could then either be very simply solved or using the solution already employed by the experimental group. The experiment supported the idea that mental set is fixed, as this group would used their established method rather than perceiving the simple solution.

WEAVER++ (Word-form Encoding by Activation and Verification) – (Levelt, 1989; Levelt et al., 1999)

Speech production occurs because there is an activation-spreading network that involves lexical concepts and nodes for abstract words (lemmas), derived from a mental dictionary, and where there are nodes containing general units of meaning (morphemes) and sounds (phonemics). According to this model, speech is produced once the following series of processes have taken place: Firstly, conceptual preparation and lexical selection; secondly, morphological, phonological, phonetic, and phonemic encoding; and, finally, encoding. In other words, general meaning leads to the processing of abstract words which then help to select basic word forms, following which, syllables are compiled, speech sounds prepared and then the actual word is produced. Initially, therefore, the mental dictionary allows a decision about word production and then specific details concerning syllables and pronunciation follow.

Word identification technique

Involves deciding whether letters make up a word (hence word identification) and then saying it aloud.

Working memory model (WMM)

A model of memory proposed by Baddeley and Hitch to replace the concept of the STM. It instead proposes separate stores of memory, controlled by a central executive, that are responsible for processing auditory and visual data. The central executive is an attentional system that has a limited capacity and is involved in decision making, together with the two slave systems (the articulatory – phonological loop and the visuo spatial scratch pad). This model is concerned with both active processing and the brief storage of information

Zoom theories

Eriksen & St James (1986) instead proposed that attention is more like a zoom lens which can be adjusted to cover a large area in much detail or a small area in specific detail, so the size of visual field that is attended to can vary.

Allport, D. A. (1989). Visual attention. In Hill, G. (2001). *A level psychology through diagrams* (p. 113). Oxford: Oxford University Press.

Anzai, Y., & Simon, H. A. (1979). The theory of learning by doing. *Psychological Review, 86,* 124–180.

Atkinson, R. C., & Shiffrin, R. M. (1968). Human memory: A proposed system and its control processes. In Spence, K. W., & Spence, J. T. *The psychology of learning & motivation.* London: Academic Press.

Baddeley, A. (1966). Short term memory for word sequences as a function of acoustic, semantic and formal similarity. *Quarterly Journal of Experimental Psychology, 18,* 362–365.

Baddeley, A. (1982). In Eysenck, M. W., & Keane, M. T. (2000). *Cognitive psychology: A student's handbook* (4th ed.) (p. 179). Hove, UK: Psychology Press.

Baddeley, A. D. (1986). *Working memory.* Oxford: Clarendon Press.

Baddeley, A. D., & Hitch, G. J. (1974). In Eysenck, M. W., & Keane, M. T. (2000). *Cognitive psychology: A student's handbook* (4th ed.) (p. 178). Hove, UK: Psychology Press.

Baddeley, A. D., Thomson, N., & Buchanan, M. (1975). Word length and the structure of STM. *Journal of Verbal Learning and Verbal Behaviour, 14,* 575–589.

Baron, J. (1997). Biases in the quantitative measurement of values for public decisions. *Psychological Bulletin, 122,* 72–88.

Bartlett, F. C. (1932). *Remembering.* Cambridge: Cambridge University Press.

Berry, D. C., & Broadbent, D. E. (1984). On the relationship between task performance & associated verbalisable knowledge. *Quarterly Journal of Experimental Psychology, 36A,* 209–231.

Biederman, I. (1987). Recognition-by-components: A theory of human image understanding. *Psychological Review, 94,* 115–147.

Blakemore, C., & Cooper, G. F. (1970). Development of the brain depends on the visual environment. *Nature, 228,* 477–478.

Braine, M. D. S., & O' Brien, D. P. (1991). A theory of If: A lexical entry, reasoning program and pragmatic principles. *Psychological Review, 98,* 182–203.

Broadbent, D. E. (1958). *Perception and communication*. Oxford: Pergamon.

Bruce, V., & Young, A. W. (1986). Understanding face recognition. *British Journal of Psychology, 77*, 305–327.

Bruner, J. S. (1956). On perceptual readiness. *Psychological Review, 63*, 123–152.

Bruno, N., & Cutting, J. E. (1988). Mini-modularity and the perception of layout. *Journal of Experimental Psychology: General, 117*, 161–170.

Cherry, E. C. (1953). Some experiments on the recognition of speech with one and two ears. *Journal of the Acoustic Society of America, 25*, 975–979.

Chomsky, N. (1956). *Syntactic structures*. The Hague: Mouton.

Christensen-Szalanski, J. J. J., & Bushyhead, J. B. (1981). Physicians' use of probabilistic information in a real clinical setting. *Journal of Experimental Psychology: Human Perception & Performance, 7*, 928–935.

Coltheart, M., Curtis, B., Atkins, P., & Haller, M. (1993). Models of reading aloud: Dual-route and parallel-distributed-processing approaches. *Psychological Review, 100*, 589–608.

Coolican, H. (1990). *Research methods and statistics in* Psychology (2nd ed.). London: Hodder and Stoughton.

Cosmides, L. (1989). The logic of social exchange: Has natural selction shaped how humans reason? *Cognition, 31*, 187–276.

Dell, G. S. (1986). A spreading-activation theory of retrieval in sentence production. *Psychological Review, 93*, 283–321.

Dell, G. S., & O'Seaghdha, P. G. (1991). Mediated and convergent lexical priming in language production: A comment on Levelt et al. (1991). *Psychological Review, 98*, 604–614.

Dell, G. S., Schwartz, M. F., Martin, N., Saffran, E. M., & Gagnon, D. A. (1997). Lexical access in aphasic and non-aphasic speakers. *Psychological Review, 104*, 801–838.

Deutsch, J. A., & Deutsch, D. (1963). Attention: Some theoretical considerations. *Psychological Review, 70*, 283–321.

Duncan, J., & Humphreys, G. W. (1989). A resemblance theory of visual search. *Psychological Review, 96*, 433–458.

Duncan, J., & Humphreys, G. W. (1992). Beyond the search surface: Visual search and attentional engagement. *Journal of Experimental Psychology: Human Perception & Performance, 18*, 578–588.

Ebbinghaus, H. (1885). In Eysenck, M. W., & Keane, M. T. (2000). *Cognitive psychology: A student's handbook* (4th ed.) (p. 169). Hove, UK: Psychology Press.

Ellis, A. W., & Young, A. W. (1988). *Human cognitive neuropsychology*. Hove, UK: Psychology Press.

Eriksen, C. W., & St James, J. D. (1986). Visual attention within and around the field of focal attention: A zoom lens model. *Perception and Psychophysics, 40*, 225–240.

Eysenck, M. W. (1984). *A handbook of cognitive psychology.* Hove, UK: Psychology Press.

Eysenck, M.W., & Flanagan, C. (2000). *Psychology for A2 level.* Hove, UK: Psychology Press.

Eysenck, M. W., & Keane, M. T. (2000). *Cognitive psychology: A student's handbook* (4th ed.). Hove, UK: Psychology Press.

Fantz, R. L. (1961). The origin of form perception. *Scientific American, 204,* 66–72.

Farah, M. J., & McClelland, J. L. (1991). A computational model of semantic memory impairment: Modality specificity and emergent category specificity. *Journal of Experimental Psychology: General, 120,* 339–357.

Frazier, L., & Rayner, K. (1982). Making and correcting errors in the analysis of structurally ambiguous sentences. *Cognitive Psychology, 14,* 178–210.

Frost, R. (1988). Toward a strong phonological theory of visual word recognition: True issues and false trails. *Psychological Bulletin, 123,* 71–99.

Gardiner, J. M., & Java, R. I. (1993). In Eysenck, M. W., & Keane, M. T. (2000). *Cognitive psychology: A student's handbook* (4th ed.) (p. 180). Hove, UK: Psychology Press.

Gibson, E. J., & Walk, R. D. (1960). The visual cliff. *Scientific American, 202,* 64–71.

Gibson, J. J. (1950). *The perception of the visual world.* Boston: Houghton Mifflin.

Gibson, J. J. (1966). The *senses considered as perceptual systems.* Boston: Houghton Mifflin.

Gibson, J. J. (1979). *The ecological approach to visual perception.* Boston: Houghton Mifflin.

Gigerenzer, G. (1996). On narrow norms and vague heuristics: A reply to Kahneman and Tversky (1996). *Psychological Review 103,* 592–596.

Graesser, A. C., Singer, M., & Trabasso, T. (1994). Constructing inferences during narrative text comprehension. *Psychological Review, 101,* 371–395.

Gray, J. A., & Wedderburn, A. A. (1960). Grouping strategies with simultaneous stimuli. *Quarterly Journal of Experimental Psychology, 12,* 180–184.

Gregory, R. L. (1972). Seeing as thinking. *Times Literary Supplement,* June 1924.

Grice, H. P. (1967). In Eysenck, M. W., & Keane, M. T. (2000). *Cognitive psychology: A student's handbook* (4th ed.) (p. 363). Hove, UK: Psychology Press.

Hayes S. R. & Simon, H. A. (1977). In Eysenck, M. W., & Keane, M. T. (2000). *Cognitive psychology: A student's handbook* (4th ed.) (p. 404). Hove, UK: Psychology Press.

Helmholtz, H. (1866). In Eysenck, M. W., & Flanagan, C. (2001) (pp. 276–277). *Psychology for A2 level.* Hove, UK: Psychology Press.

Hering, E. (1878). In Eysenck, M. W., & Flanagan, C. (2001) (p. 277). *Psychology for A2 level*. Hove, UK: Psychology Press.

Hill, G. (2001). *A level psychology through diagrams*. Oxford: Oxford university press.

Hitch, G., & Baddeley, A. D. (1976). Verbal reasoning and working memory. *Quarterly Journal of Experimental Psychology, 28*, 603–621.

Humphreys, G. W., Lamote, C., & Lloyd-Jones, T. J. (1995). An interactive activation approach to object processing: Effects of structural similarity, name frequency and task in normality and pathology, *Memory, 3*, 535–586.

Janowsky, J. S., Shimamura, A. P., & Squire, L. R. (1989). Source memory impairment in patients with frontal lobe lesions. *Neuropsychologia, 27*, 1043–1056.

Jenkins, J. G., & Dallenbach, K. M. (1924). Obliviscence during sleep and waking. *American Journal of Psychology, 35*, 605–612.

Johnson, M. K., Hashtroudi, S., & Lindsay, D. S. (1993). Source monitoring. *Psychological Bulletin, 114*, 3–28.

Johnston, W. A., & Heinz, S. P. (1978). Flexibility and capacity demands of attention. *Journal of Experimental Psychology: General, 107*, 420–435.

Johnston, W. A., & Wilson, J. A. (1980). Perceptual processing of non-targets in an attention task. *Memory and Cognition, 8*, 372–377.

Jones, G. V. (1982). In Eysenck, M. W., & Keane, M. T. (2000). *Cognitive psychology: A student's handbook* (4th ed.) (p. 180). Hove, UK: Psychology Press.

Just, M. A., & Carpenter, P. A. (1992). A capacity theory of comprehension: New frontiers of evidence and arguments. *Psychological Review, 103*, 773–780.

Kahneman, D. (1973). *Attention & effort*. Englewood Cliffs, NJ: Prentice-Hall.

Kahneman, D., & Tversky, A. (1973). On the psychology of prediction. *Psychological Review, 80*, 237–251.

Kahneman, D., & Tversky, A. (1984). Choices, values and frames. *American Psychologist, 39*, 341–350.

Kintsch. W, (1988). The role of knowledge in discourse comprehension: A construction-integration model. *Psychological Review, 95*, 163–182.

Kintsch, W. (1992). In Eysenck, M. W., & Keane, M. T. (2000). *Cognitive psychology: A student's handbook* (4th edition) (p. 357). Hove, UK: Psychology Press.

Kintsch, W. (1994). In Eysenck, M. W., & Keane, M. T. (2000). *Cognitive psychology: A student's handbook* (4th ed.) (p. 357). Hove, UK: Psychology Press.

Kintsch, W., & Van Dijk, T. A. (1978). Toward a model of text comprehension and production. *Psychological Review, 85*, 363–394.

Koehler, J. J. (1996). In Eysenck, M. W., & Keane, M. T. (2000). *Cognitive psychology: A student's handbook* (4th ed.) (p. 477). Hove, UK: Psychology Press.

Koffka, K. (1935). *Principles of Gestalt psychology*. New York: Harcourt Brace.

Kohler, W. (1927). In Eysenck, M. W., & Keane, M. T. (2000). *Cognitive psychology: A student's handbook* (4th ed.) (p. 396). Hove, UK: Psychology Press.

Kohler, W. (1927). *The Mentality of Apes* (2nd ed.). New York: Harcourt Brace.

Kotovsky, K. Hayes, J. R., & Simon, H. A. (1985). Why are some problems hard? Evidence from the Tower of Hanoi. *Cognitive Psychology, 17*, 248–294.

Levelt, W. J. M. (1989). *Speaking: From intention to articulation*. Cambridge, MA: MIT Press.

Levelt, W. J. M., Roelofs, A., & Meyer, A. S. (1999). A theory of lexical access in speech production. *Behavioural & Brain Sciences, 22*, 1–38.

Liberman, A. M., Cooper, F. S., Shankweiler, D. S., & Studdert-Kennedy, M. (1967). Perception of the speech code. *Psychological Review, 74*, 431–461.

Logie, R. H. (1995). *Visuo-spatial working memory*. Hove, UK: Psychology Press.

Logie, R. H. (1999). In Eysenck, M. W., & Keane, M. T. (2000). *Cognitive psychology: A student's handbook* (4th ed.) (p. 156). Hove, UK: Psychology Press.

Luchins, A. S., & Luchins, E. H. (1959). *Rigidity of behaviour*. Eugene, OR: University of Oregon Press.

MacDonald, M. C., Perlmutter, N. J., & Seidenberg, M. S. (1994). Lexical nature of syntactic ambiguity resolution. *Psychological Review, 101*, 676–703.

Maier, N. R. F. (1931). Reasoning in humans II: The solution of a problem and its appearance in consciousness. *Journal of Comparative Psychology, 12*, 181–194.

Marcus, S., & Rips, L. J. (1979). Conditional reasoning. *Journal of Verbal Learning & Verbal Behaviour, 18*, 199–233.

Marr, D. (1982). *Vision: A computational investigation into the human representation and processing of visual information*. San Francisco: W. H. Freeman.

Marr, D. & Nishihara, k. (1978). Representation and Recognition of the spatial organisation of three-dimensional shapes. *Philosophical Transactions of the Royal Society, Series B*, 269–294.

Marslen-Wilson, W. D. (1990). In Eysenck, M. W., & Keane, M. T. (2000). *Cognitive psychology: A student's handbook* (4th ed.) (p. 311). Hove, UK: Psychology Press.

Marslen-Wilson, W. D., & Tyler, L. K. (1980). The temporal structure of spoken language comprehension. *Cognition, 6*, 1–71.

Marslen-Wilson, W. D., & Warren, P. (1994). Levels of perceptual representation and process in lexical access: Words, phonemes, and features. *Psychological Review, 101*, 653–675.

McClelland, J. L. (1991). Stochastic interactive processes and the effect of context on perception. *Cognitive Psychology, 23*, 1–44.

McClelland, J. L., & Elman, J. L. (1986). The TRACE model of speech perception. *Cognitive Psychology, 18,* 1–86.

McClelland, J. L., & Rumelhart, D. E. (1981). An interactive activation model of context effects in letter perception. Part 1. An account of basic findings. *Psychological Review, 88,* 375–407.

McIlroy, D. (2003) *Studying at university: How to be a successful student.* London: Sage.

McKoon, G., & Ratcliff, R. (1986). In Eysenck, M.W., & Keane, M.T. (2000) *Cognitive psychology: A student's handbook* (4th ed.) (p 348). Hove, UK: Psychology Press.

McKoon, G., & Ratcliff, R. (1992). Inference during reading. *Psychological Review, 99,* 440–466.

Miller, G. A. (1956).The magical number seven, plus or minus two: Some limits on our capacity for processing information. *Psychological Review, 63,* 81–97.

Minter, P. (1978). Recognition failure. In Eysenck, M. W., & Keane, M. T. (2000). *Cognitive psychology: A student's handbook* (4th ed.) (p. 178). Hove, UK: Psychology Press.

Murdock, B. B. (1962) In Gross, R. D., & McIlveen, R. (1998). *Psychology: A new introduction.* (pp. 232–233). London: Hodder & Stoughton.

Muter, P. (1978). Recognition failure of recallable words in semantic memory. *Memory and cognition, 6,* 9–12.

Navon, D. (1977). Forest before trees: The precedence of global features in visual perception. *Cognitive Psychology, 9,* 353–383.

Neisser, U. (1964). Visual search. *Scientific American, 210,* 94–102.

Neisser, U. (1976). *Cognition & reality.* San Francisco: W. H. Freeman.

Neumann, J.& Morgenstern, O.(1947). In Eysenck, M. W., & Keane, M. T. (2000). *Cognitive psychology: A student's handbook* (4th ed.) (p. 483). Hove, UK: Psychology Press.

Newell, A., & Simon, H. A. (1972). *Human problem solving.* Englewood Cliffs, NJ: Prentice-Hall.

Oaksford, M. R., & Chater, N. (1994). A rational analysis of the selection task as optimal data selection. *Psychological Review, 101,* 608–631.

Oaksford, M. R., & Chater (1995). Information gain explains relevance which explains the selection task. *Cognition, 57,* 97–108.

Oaksford, M. R., & Chater (1996). Rational explanation of the selection task. *Psychological Review, 103,* 381–391.

Ohlsson, S (1992). In Eysenck, M. W., & Keane, M. T. (2000). *Cognitive psychology: A student's handbook* (4th ed.) (p. 399). Hove, UK: Psychology Press.

Peterson, L. R., & Peterson, M. (1959). Short term retention of individual verbal items. *Journal of Experimental Psychology, 58,* 193–198.

Piaget, J. (1932). *The moral judgement of the child.* Harmondsworth, UK: Penguin.

Plaut, D. C., McClelland, J. L., Seidenberg, M. S., & Patterson, K. (1996). Understanding normal and impaired word reading: Computational principles in quasi-regular domains. *Psychological Review, 103,* 56–115.

Rayner, K., & Sereno, S. C. (1994). In Eysenck, M. W., & Keane, M. T. (2000). *Cognitive psychology: A student's handbook* (4th ed.) (p. 321). Hove, UK: Psychology Press.

Reichle, E. D., Pollatsek, A., Fisher, D.L. & Rayner, K. (1998). Towards a model of eye movement control in reading. *Psychological Review, 105,* 125–157.

Rottenstreich, Y., & Tversky, A. (1997). Unpacking, repacking, and anchoring: Advances in support theory. *Psychological Review, 104,* 406–415.

Schank, R. C. (1976). In Eysenck, M. W., & Keane, M. T. (2000). *Cognitive psychology: A student's handbook* (4th ed.) (p. 168). Hove, UK: Psychology Press.

Schank, R. C., & Abelson, R. P. (1977). *Scripts, plans, goals and understanding.* Hillsdale, NJ: Lawrence Erlbaum.

Schneider, W., & Shiffrin, R. M. (1977). Controlled & automatic human information processing: 1. detention, search & attention. *Psychological Review, 84,* 1–66.

Seger, C. A. (1994). In Eysenck, M. W., & Keane, M. T. (2000). *Cognitive psychology: A student's handbook* (4th ed.) (p. 63). Hove, UK: Psychology Press.

Selfridge, O. G. (1959). Pandemonium: A paradigm for learning. In Eysenck, M. W., & Flanagan, C. (2001). *Psychology for A2 level* (p. 257). Hove, UK: Psychology Press.

Shanks, D. R., & St John M. F. (1994). Characteristics of dissociable human learning systems. *Behavioural & Brain Sciences, 17,* 367–394.

Simon, H. A., & Reed, S. K. (1976). Modelling strategy shifts on a problem solving task. *Cognitive Psychology, 8,* 86–97.

Sperling, G. (1960). The information that is available in brief visual presentations. *Psychological Monographs, 74* (whole no. 498), 1–29.

Thompson, D.M., & Tulving, E. (1970). Associative encoding and retrieval: weak and strong cues. *Journal of Experimental Psychology, 86,* 255–262.

Thompson, D. M., & Tulving, E. (1978). In Eysenck, M. W., & Keane, M. T. (2000). *Cognitive psychology: A student's handbook* (4th ed.) (p.176). Hove, UK: Psychology Press.

Treisman, A. M. (1960). Contextual cues in selective listening. *Quarterly Journal of Experimental Psychology, 12,* 242–248.

Treisman, A. M. (1988). Features and objects: The fourteenth Bartlett memorial lecture. *Quarterley Journal of Experimental Psychology, 40A,* 201–237.

Treisman, A. M. (1992). Spreading suppression or failure integration? A reply to Duncan & Humphreys (1992). *Journal of Experimental Psychology: Human Perception & Performance, 18,* 589–593.

Treisman, A. M., & Riley, J. G. A. (1969). Is selective attention selective perception or selective response: A further test. *Journal of Experimental Psychology 79* 27–34.

Tulving, E. (1972). In Eysenck, M. W., & Keane, M. T. (2000). *Cognitive psychology: A student's handbook* (4th ed.) (p. 202). Hove, UK: Psychology Press.

Tulving, E. (1983). *Elements of episodic memory*. Oxford: Oxford University Press.

Tversky, A., & Kahneman, D. (1973). Availability: A heuristic for judging frequency and probability. *Cognitive Psychology, 5*, 207–232.

Tversky, A., & Kahneman, D. (1974). Judgement under uncertainty: Heuristics and biases. *Science, 185*, 1124–1131.

Tversky, A., & Kahneman, D. (1980). In Eysenck, M. W., & Keane, M. T. (2000). *Cognitive psychology: A student's handbook* (4th ed.) (p. 477). Hove, UK: Psychology Press.

Tversky, A., & Kahneman, D. (1987). In Eysenck, M. W., & Keane, M. T. (2000). *Cognitive psychology: A student's handbook* (4th ed.) (p. 484). Hove, UK: Psychology Press.

Tversky, A., & Koehler, D. J. (1994). Support theory: A nonextensional representation of subjective probability. *Psychological Review, 101*, 547–567.

Tversky, A., & Shafir, E. (1992). The disjunction effect in choice under uncertainty. *Psychological Science, 3*, 305–309.

Watkins, M. J., & Gardiner, J. M. (1979). An appreciation of generate-recognise theory of recall. *Journal of Verbal Learning & Verbal Behaviour, 18*, 687–704.

Waugh, N. C., & Norman, D. A. (1965). Primary memory. *Psychological Review, 72*, 89–104

Wheeler, M. A., Stuss, D. T., & Tulving, E. (1997). Toward a theory of episodic memory: The frontal lobes and autonoetic consciousness. *Psychological Bulletin, 121*, 331–354.

Williams, L. M. (1994). Recall of childhood trauma: A prospective study of women's memories of child abuse. *Journal of Consulting & Clinical Psychology, 62*, 1167–1176.

Wolfe, J. M. (1998). In Eysenck, M. W., & Keane, M. T. (2000). *Cognitive psychology: A student's handbook* (4th ed.) (p. 131). Hove, UK: Psychology Press.

Zwaan, R. A., & Radvansky, G. A. (1990). Situation models in language comprehension and memory. *Psychological Bulletin, 123*, 162–185.